F·R·O·M
ASHES
T·O
GLORY

Conflict and victories on and
beyond the football field

F·R·O·M
ASHES
T·O
GLORY

Bill McCartney
with Dave Diles

THOMAS NELSON PUBLISHERS
Nashville

Published in Nashville, Tennessee, by Thomas Nelson, Inc., and distributed in Canada by Lawson Falle, Ltd., Cambridge, Ontario.

Scripture quotations, unless noted, are from the NEW KING JAMES VERSION of the Bible. Copyright © 1979, 1980, 1982, Thomas Nelson, Inc., Publishers.

Scripture quotations noted NIV are from the HOLY BIBLE: NEW INTERNATIONAL VERSION. Copyright © 1973, 1978, 1984 by the International Bible Society. Used by permission of Zondervan Bible Publishers.

Library of Congress Cataloging-in-Publication Data:

McCartney, Bill,
    From ashes to glory/Bill McCartney with Dave Diles.
      p. cm.
    ISBN 0-8407-7577-6
    1. McCartney, Bill.   2. Football—United States—Coaches—Biography.
    3. University of Colorado, Boulder—Football—History.
    I. Diles, David L.   II. Title.
GV939, M298A3 1990   90-38980
796.332'092—dc20   CIP
[B]

Printed in the United States of America
1 2 3 4 5 6 7 — 95 94 93 92 91 90

Dedication

This book is written in the hope that it will light one path, lift one spirit, stir one heart and awaken one soul.

It is dedicated to Lyndi McCartney, who has given so much love, provided so much care and dedication and made so many sacrifices; to the McCartney children, Mike, Tom, Kristyn and Marc and to little Timothy Chase, for being loving and understanding enough so that one dream could be pursued.

And it is dedicated to the late Lucille and Lisle Diles who lived, rather than preached, their sermons and who never once cursed the darkness.

Bill McCartney
and Dave Diles

Other Books by Dave Diles:

Duffy

Nobody's Perfect

Twelfth Man in the Huddle

Archie

Terry Bradshaw—Man of Steel

Up Close and Personal:
The Inside Story of Network Television Sports

Acknowledgements

The authors wish to thank the members of the University of Colorado family—President E. Gordon Gee, athletic director Bill Marolt, sports information director Dave Plati and special assistant Rick George for their assistance in providing access to information for this book. We are particularly grateful to Coach McCartney's secretary, Judy Wolf.

This would have been an incomplete story without the cooperation of Eddie Crowder, Bo Schembechler, Joe Schmidt, Jon Falk, Theo Gregory and Dr. Will Miles, whose recollections added insight and understanding. Particular thanks go to Hal Nees of the Boulder Police Department, and Dave Evans of the University of Colorado Police Department.

A special tribute is due members of the McCartney family—Lyndi, Mike, Tom, Kristyn and Marc—for understanding the importance of sharing the very soul of Bill McCartney through excerpts from his daily journal, sprinkled liberally throughout these pages. Without this journal, the reader could never comprehend either the strength and courage, or the fears and frailties of the man about whom we write.

Bill Kuecher and David Allen gave invaluable guidance and counsel when we most needed it, and Anne Dix put all else on the back burner to devote her time and talents to this work.

We are most grateful for the confidence and trust placed in us by Bruce Barbour. We gathered great strength from an old friend, Ron Haynes, who steered this ship through some perilous waters, and were encouraged by the skills of our editor, Karen Scalf Linamen.

Dave Diles
Racine, Ohio

Table of Contents

Introduction

When the question of my getting the job as head football coach at the University of Colorado was still unsettled, I made it clear to those doing the hiring that football was not the number one priority in my life. I explained that it was God first, family second, and football third.

And nothing has changed.

Only when our football program received national acclaim did the opportunity arise to write this book. After all, no one pays much attention to losers.

So I am most grateful for the glorious victories. But I am thankful, too, for the defeats. I am convinced that without the setbacks on the field, our program at Colorado would never have endured the hardships and thrived. Just as surely, I am persuaded that without the adversities in the personal lives of the McCartney family, I would have had neither the strength, courage nor the wisdom to write this book.

Hopefully, the reader will not view this effort as just another book about another football coach. Like my co-author, I am "in" what the world calls the jock culture—but not "of it." There is much more to my life, much more to the lives of the young men who have been a part of our struggle, than the mere winning and losing of football games. MacArthur told us that upon the fields of friendly strife are sown the seeds that in other battles, in later life, will bear the fruits of victory.

I have no problem with exposing myself to the world for what I really am. I'm an ordinary guy with an extraordinary God. I want to share with everyone the struggles I have been through, struggles that reinforced rather than sapped my belief that God is faithful. There is no hesitation about telling the truth, no apprehension about sharing my fears and my doubts.

I am not afraid to tell the world that I have a struggle with alcohol; that I have a battle with my temper; that I agonize over things that are said and written about me and my family; that I second-guess myself a lot, that I wonder whether I am worthy; that I have feelings of guilt.

My primary purpose in writing this book is to share the Gospel and to show how the Word of God affects someone under the microscope, under the pressures of big-time athletics. I understand that in doing this, I will place myself and those I love under even closer scrutiny, and that's all right, too. I do not anticipate that everyone will receive this book in the spirit in which it is written, but sometimes one has to pay an extraordinary price for sharing what is in one's heart. I know that I am vulnerable, but that makes me useful to God.

If someone says, "Oh, another Jesus freak, here we go again!" I'll understand. I am not ashamed of the Gospel of Jesus Christ. I don't want to cram my beliefs down anybody's throat, but I must proclaim my faith. If I do not proclaim Christ before men, He won't proclaim me before His Father in Heaven. I must not be intimidated lest I offend someone, else I wouldn't be God's man.

Bill McCartney
Boulder, Colorado

Chronology of Events

June 10, 1982	Bill is hired head coach at Colorado University.
September 15, 1984	Ed Reinhardt receives injury in game against Oregon University, ending a promising football career.
October 1984	Athletic Director Bill Marolt fuels controversy when he renews McCartney's contract in middle of 1-10 season.
November 17, 1984	Colorado program hits rock botton with loss to Kansas State, 38-6.
Season of 1985	Beginning with opening game of the season, Buffaloes begin to build on a foundation laid during the past three years, concluding season with 7-4 record and drawing unprecedented national attention.
February 12, 1986	Bill recruits Sal Aunese from Oceanside, California
October 25, 1986	Colorado beats Nebraska, ending 20-year losing streak against the Cornhuskers.
Season of 1987	7-4 record leaves Buffaloes trailing the best teams in the conference in a "just miss" season.
August 31, 1988	Bill begins keeping personal journal.

December 29, 1988	Colorado plays in Freedom Bowl; loses to Brigham Young.
January 1989	Controversy rages as Bill considers breaking contract with Colorado to rebuild football program at SMU.
March 29, 1989	Bill learns that Sal Aunese is dying of cancer.
April 4, 1989	Kristyn McCartney gives birth to Timothy Chase.
July 22, 1989	Bill leads Sal Aunese to Jesus Christ.
August 21, 1989	Pastor Ryle prophesies of Buff's "Golden Season."
August 30, 1989	*Westword* article devastates McCartney family.
September 23, 1989	Sal dies of cancer.
January 1, 1990	Colorado meets Notre Dame in the 1990 Orange Bowl.

One

Miracle
in Miami

Finally, the day was here. In a matter of hours—if we beat Notre Dame in the 1990 Orange Bowl—the University of Colorado Buffaloes would be the undisputed national champions of college football.

The bus ride to the stadium was short. We had stayed in a Marriott Hotel away from our fans and family the night before the game, in an effort to control the circus, to focus, to concentrate. I had learned, as an assistant coach under Bo Schembechler at Michigan, that when you're on the threshold of a major game, family and friends can rob a team of its concentration. So I had made the decision weeks ahead of time: we'd spend the eve of the game at a different hotel to try and orchestrate a smooth and uneventful lead-in to the game.

None of us expected much as the bus rumbled toward the tunnel where we would exit and make our way to the locker rooms.

Then, suddenly, players and coaches were standing in their seats, pointing, craning their necks for a better view as the bus began to grind to a halt.

I'll never forget what we saw: Buffalo fans were lined up eight to ten deep to greet us. Our bus rolled into a virtual canyon created by two walls of human bodies. And they were cheering. More than cheering, they were feverish. Electric.

Usually I try not to allow myself to indulge in this kind of pre-game hype, but this time it felt different. I tried to catch my breath and present a poised game face, while inside I wanted to hug and grab and slap high-fives with every man, woman and child cheering us on.

I was sky high walking into that locker room. And I wasn't the only one.

The atmosphere in the locker room was subdued, with game faces tightening as the athletes dressed. I looked at my watch. It was six in the evening.

Two hours left to go before the game.

I think if you polled college coaches and players, they would tell you decisively that they prefer day games to evening contests. Especially when it is a major game.

When the game is slated for evening—like our Orange Bowl contest against Notre Dame—the day drags by, the approaching game consumes you and you look for *anything* to occupy your time and ease the anxiety that lies in heavy knots in the pit of your stomach.

I had worried that the day would be like that for me. But it wasn't. And maybe part of the reason for that was an early morning visit I'd received from Jim Schultz.

Jim had coached with me at Dearborn Divine Child High School in the early '70s. For almost three hours that morning, we had reminisced about times past and where our paths had taken us in life. Jim had eventually gone into administration, and was soon to retire. I'd stayed in coaching, leaving high school athletics—what was it now?—sixteen years ago. I'd spent profitable years as an assistant coach under Bo Schembechler at the University of Michigan. And then, seven-and-a-half years ago, my wife, Lyndi, and I pulled up stakes in Michigan and came west to try to pump new life into the neglected football program at the University of Colorado.

As Jim and I reminisced, I couldn't help but recall the day the Colorado football program hit rock bottom.

I still can't explain why I couldn't get that game out of my mind, except that perhaps football really is like everything else in life, where it's often true that you cannot begin to climb until you've hit the absolute bottom.

And Colorado football hit it on November 17, 1984, at Manhattan, Kansas. For Kansas State to beat Colorado—that's bad enough—but we got trounced 38-6. And we even looked terrible in defeat: I mean, it's undeniably humiliating when you're losing 24-0, you score your only touchdown of the game, try an onside kick and the other team runs it back for their fourth touchdown!

I thought back to how I'd felt the next morning in Boulder, when I picked up the Sunday newspaper and found, splashed across the pages, that one of our best players, wide receiver Loy Alexander, had put our entire program under severe attack. McCartney was recruiting choir boys, he said, not football players. It was a take-off on the old line credited to Leo Durocher that "Nice guys finish last." Alexander said we had enough nice guys; what we needed, and didn't have enough of, were tough and aggressive young men who could play football. Loy said that Colorado's program wasn't going to get any better because the players I had recruited simply weren't good enough to win in the Big Eight Conference.

Even our most ardent supporters had been rattled by Alexander's criticism. They had been clinging to what I had promised them—that we were laying a foundation that would stand the test of time. But I knew on that Sunday morning, Colorado fans reading that article wouldn't remember much of what I'd been say-ing about having to dig deeply so we could build high.

Alexander's remarks had a long-lasting effect. They hurt our recruiting the following year. High school seniors read those criticisms—recruiters from other schools made sure of that.

The day Loy's criticisms hit the headlines, I was to speak at the Minnesota Vikings' chapel service before they played the Broncos in Denver. As I drove to Denver, I felt humiliated by the headlines, and I wondered what the Minnesota players would think, and how they'd respond to a coach who'd just directed his team to a 1-10 season and been raked over the coals by one of his star players. It was a low moment for me—and the Viking players couldn't have felt they were getting any bargain, either.

Those had been dark times, indeed.

But recalling them, spending time with Jim Schultz—in a Miami hotel room, getting ready to play for the national championship—had made the hours before the Orange Bowl contest even sweeter.

Reminiscing with Jim had reminded me of something else, too: I remembered how Lyndi and I had flown back to Michigan a few years ago when Jim and his wife lost one of their daughters in a tragic accident. Kristin Schultz and one of her friends died because a neighbor's hot tub wasn't properly ventillated. It was a terrible, terrible time for both families.

And I remembered how—when trouble visited *my* home and *my* beautiful daughter, beginning eighteen months ago in August of 1988—it was the memory of Jim and Ellen Schultz and their loss that had made my troubles seem a whole lot smaller.

Our adversities—losing seasons, stumbling blocks, my short-comings as a coach, personal tragedies and even death—these were the things that made just being there, in Miami, seem like such a miracle. It wasn't a matter of getting even, or of proving something to someone else as much as it was knowing, down deep, that our task had been worthy, that people had embraced each other in a noble effort and had seen it through.

Hours before our moment of contest—before our chance of a lifetime in the 1990 Orange Bowl—my exhilaration mingled with bittersweet reflections. No one could say it had been an easy journey to the top. Professionally, and personally, too, it seemed as though the past seven years couldn't have held more heartache.

Or greater challenge. . .

Two

Yea, Though I Walk Through the Valley. . .

On the last day of August, 1988, I began keeping a daily journal.

It was the start of my seventh year at the University of Colorado. We were well into a long-term rebuilding program and beginning to see some results, but still a year-and-a-half—and an uphill climb—from the 1990 Orange Bowl. The burdens I carried—at that point, at least—weren't all that heavier than those borne by many other coaches. So when I came up with the idea to begin a journal, it wasn't for reasons any nobler than the fact that I liked the idea of having somewhere to put my thoughts.

Not in my wildest dreams could I have imagined that my journals would document the gripping events that they did. . .or that we would soon draw fire and praise from the national media. . .or that my family and my players would face the things we were about to face. . .

But it was as if someone knew these things. . .as if I were somehow being prepared for what lay just around the corner. Because just about the time I began my journals, my nineteen-year-old daughter made a discovery—one that would have implications reaching as far as the national press and on into eternity.

Kristyn discovered she was two-months pregnant by Sal Aunese, star quarterback of the Buffaloes—the team that I coached.

Her heart no doubt pounding double-time, Kristy knew she needed to break the news to Sal. On Sunday, she showed up at the house where he lived with several other students. She found a crowd gathered in the living room, watching a football game on TV. She caught Sal's attention and drew close for privacy.

"I have something to tell you," she said in a low voice. "In private."

Sal gave up the easy chair in front of the tube and led the way past the kitchen and into one of the bedrooms. He closed the door behind them.

Kristy bit her lip, eyeing Sal briefly before she spoke. Finally she said, "You're not going to be happy about this. You're going to be really mad at me. I'm pregnant."

Sal stared a moment, letting the words soak in. Finally, he nodded. "Okay. So, what are you planning to do about it?"

Kristy was taken back. She swallowed. "I. . .I guess I'm going to have an abortion."

Sal took the whole thing with a shrug. What little reaction there was seemed to be one of indifference.

In a matter of days the word had spread to a close circle of Sal's friends on the team, and Sal and his friends began urging my daughter to hurry up with the abortion. "Don't tell your folks," they insisted. "This thing can be fixed quickly. . ."

Then Kristyn talked with some of her Christian friends. "Go home and tell your parents," they advised. "They love you."

Kristyn ignored the friends who warned her of the "humiliation and disgrace" that would fall on her parents if she went public with her pregnancy. Kristyn is a believer. She had already openly and publicly committed her life to Jesus Christ. Despite a moment of stolen intimacy with Sal—and the ramifications of that act—Kristy knew she was in God's hands.

And she knew she needed the support of her parents.

The following Saturday, after a game, Kristy found Lyndi and I relaxing at home in the den. She walked in and headed behind the couch where Lyndi and I sat. Kristy put one arm around my shoulder, and the other around Lyndi, holding each of us tightly.

And then she just blurted out the news: "I'm pregnant."

Suddenly Kristy was crying, and Lyndi and I were on our knees beside her, holding her, loving her.

Lyndi spoke the first words. "Are you alright?" she asked, battling her own tears.

I asked Kristyn who the father was.

Sobbing, she could barely speak the words. "Sal. Sal Aunese."

Lyndi and I had suspected

> **How I wanted to do or say something to give my beautiful daughter a lift—something to encourage her, to brighten her life. She loved Sal and she knew now he did not love her.**
> *Bill McCartney*

that our daughter was in love with Sal. The pain of Kristy's broken heart reverberated in her sobs.

In the following weeks, Lyndi and I talked to our daughter about the choices she faced. "There are a couple places in Ohio where you could have the baby," I remember saying. "Or we have friends in Ann Arbor."

Lyndi nodded, adding, "You could give the baby away in adoption—there are lots of couples that would love to have a healthy child—or you can stay here in Boulder and have the baby here. It's really whatever you want to do. It's your choice."

Neither Lyndi nor I mentioned abortion. Without question, our daughter knew our posture on abortion, but this was no time for us to make decisions for her. In truth, had abortion been Kristy's choice, we would have considered it her decision. I held my breath, waiting for my daughter's response.

Kristy squared her shoulders. "I'm going to have the baby here. In Boulder."

Here? In Boulder? It was not what I wanted her to do, because I could see the pain that lay ahead for all of us. But it was her choice to make.

"God bless you, Kristy," I told her as the three of us hugged and held each other close. "You are really something special. Do you realize what is in store for you?"

"We'll go through it together, won't we?" she asked through her tears.

I just nodded.

I suspected that the coming months would be tough, but I had no idea *how* tough. The fires of controversy would be hot, searing my family, my career, athletes on the Colorado team—and Kristyn's tearful words would take on new meaning for all of us: *We'll go through it together. . .*

And that's how it happened that I found myself writing the following words. It was September 25, the day after we had beaten Oregon State for our third straight victory of the season—and three and a half weeks after I had begun keeping my journal. I am a Christian, and as I wrote, it was only natural to turn all my thoughts—including my fears about Kristy and my joy about the Oregon victory—over to God:

> Kristy told Lyndi and me of her pregnancy. Lord, I am grateful that she had the strength and courage of character to proceed with the birth. Thank you Jesus! Lord, my heart grieves for her and Lyndi. Strengthen them both in this crisis. Lord, select a godly man for our precious daughter.
>
> And thank you for our victory yesterday on the field.

My intensity and emotion on the sidelines continue to present problems for me. Lord, I pray for self-control. I pray for wisdom in dealing with frustrated players. Lord, I thank you for a 3-0 start. Glory to you, O Lord!

It was the beginning of my seventh season coaching at the University of Colorado, having been hired out of assistant coaching days under Bo Schembechler at the University of Michigan.

When I had hired on as head coach back in '82, the word about the University of Colorado had been that football players went there to have a good time, to attend classes when they felt motivated—and that they played football on just about the same terms. Chuck Fairbanks, who a decade earlier had won big at Oklahoma, had just resigned, leaving behind a team that had won only seven games in three years. Now, at the top of my seventh year at Colorado, we were that far

Lyndi McCartney:

It's difficult for family members to cope with the adulation that an athlete, or a coach, receives. Kristy has had some difficult battles. Being the only girl in a jock world and not being particularly blessed with athletic skills, she has had to struggle to find her place of acceptance.

As athletes, each of the boys has had special moments when they have shone. Yet most of us have gifts or talents that don't receive spotlight attention. Thus, we have to learn to appreciate ourselves and live in the hope that those we truly love understand that we're contributing, too, but in a quiet way.

into a long-term rebuilding program and finally beginning to see some of the fruit of our hard work.

Three and 0. A good sign. A cause for hope.

Yet my heart was torn between celebration on the field and crisis at home.

The Tuesday following our win over Oregon, I approached Gary Barnett, Sal Aunese's position coach. I asked Coach Barnett to deliver a message from me to Sal. The message he carried was that Kristy had told Lyndi and me about the pregnancy—but that this matter was separate from football and that it would not affect our player/coach relationship. When the moment was right, I knew I would approach Sal myself. But the moment wasn't right. Not yet.

On October 1 we defeated Colorado State, boosting our record to 4 and 0. Sal threw a 13-yard touchdown pass to Mike Pritchard to win the game with only 38 seconds left to play.

I recorded the victory in my journal. Then I wrote on, recording candid thoughts about matters that were professional and, more importantly, personal:

> Lord, our squad needs strong leadership. Help me to provide it. Lord, I pray to be strong, loving and wise. Lord, Kristy is experiencing much hurt and heartache. Please show her Your perfect will.

On October 4 I admitted:

> Lord, I yield to anxiety frequently. I believe that You deeply love me and are always watching over me. Please forgive my lack of faith. Kristy is hurting. Sal still dates others.

And finally on October 5:

> Many anxious moments dot my days and nights, Lord. Is this a lack of faith? Lord, I want to rejoice in your

truths and rise above the routine anxieties of this world. Have mercy on me for my unbelieving attitudes and renew in me a strong faith that focuses on You, and not on circumstances.

I've never been a man to say less than what I really mean. So I won't say now that the weeks and months following Kristy's announcement were easy ones. Because they weren't. I hurt for Kristy. For Lyndi. For me. I hurt for Sal. I felt angry, confused and—at some level—betrayed. But I was dead set that my personal feelings wouldn't impact my role as Sal's coach, my judgment of him as a player, or my responsibility to the entire Colorado team.

Three days later we lost to Oklahoma State 41-21. We turned the ball over six times and the fine young man who would go on to win the Heisman Trophy, Barry Sanders, rushed for 174 yards and scored four touchdowns.

The next morning I wrote:

OSU 41, CU 21. Thank you, Jesus! In faith I believe that you direct our football program. Lord, lead the way. I want to carry my load. And Lord, be patient with me. Forgive me for the ways I fail you. I confess anger on the sidelines that is unhealthy and disruptive. Forgive me. I regret my behavior. Lord, I pray for strength, love and wisdom in leading our squad onward. Thank you, Lord, for Lyndi and her faithfulness. And I pray for a healthy baby inside Kristy. Lord, raise up a dynamic child of God!

It was about that time that I began to speak out publicly against abortion. Kristy's pregnancy had made me painfully aware of how easy it is for young people to point to abortion as a quick solution to a difficult problem. Many of my good and well-intentioned friends told me I was wrong to do it. But I still looked for opportunities to speak out, and got the chance to address a crowd of a thousand at a Right to Life dinner in Denver. In my heart, I knew the timing was right to take a stand. And like I said, I've never been a man to say less than what's in my heart.

About that same time, I began to realize it was the right time for something else, as well. I knew it was time for me to speak with Sal.

It would be the first time Sal and I would meet face to face on the matter of Kristy and the pregnancy. But it wouldn't be his first communication from our family on the issue. And the more I thought about what I wanted to say to Sal, the more I prayed that my words might reflect the same kind of support and unconditional love that Lyndi had managed to communicate to Sal.

You see, within days after Kristy told us about the pregnancy, Lyndi had sat down and penned a letter to the man who had broken our daughter's heart and fathered her child. It could have been a letter filled with hate. It might have brimmed with accusations. It could have relayed our fears and our hurt; could have wrought division and bitterness. Instead, this is what she wrote:

"Hi Sal,

"I wanted to talk to you in person, so I could give you a hug and let you know it's all going to be okay. I know you're hurting, too, and I know this is very scary and difficult to face. I want you to have confidence that the decisions you'll be making over the next few months will be totally acceptable no matter what they are—with two exceptions: No quitting school and no quitting the team. Those two are vital to your future and your personal well-being.

"Kristy is so deeply concerned for your future and doesn't want to hamper your success in any way. We feel the same and I hope this letter will convey warm feelings and no judgments.

"Coach Mac and I think you are a terrific person and it is not our desire to pressure you or take anything away from you or even punish you in any way. What you and Kristy are experiencing is life. Perhaps it's not what either of you planned, but a moment of passion has created a miracle within Kristy and I know that within Kristy's heart, that moment was filled with love. 'Many are the plans in a man's heart, but it is the Lord's purpose that prevails.' (NIV Prov. 19:21)

"Now that the Lord has your attention and Kristy's attention, you must realize that this beautiful child belongs to God. In other words, that's God's baby. Don't mess with God's baby! And you know what else? You're God's baby, too. So is Kristy and you both deserve lots of tender love and care. Spending time with the Lord, getting to know Him in an intimate way will increase your faith and fill you with peace. Loving Jesus will calm your fears and give you strength, but it won't make problems go away, it won't keep pain and suffering from your life because pain and suffering have a purpose in life. 'If you remain indifferent in times of adversity, your strength will depart from you.' (NIV Prov. 24:10)

"Sal, you need to share this with your family. They love you and wouldn't want you to go through this alone. You're their baby, no matter how grown up you are, and your well-being means everything in the world to them. Of course, I can't guarantee their immediate reaction but I know in the long term, you'll have their love and support and that's pretty wonderful. I would never interfere with your personal decision. I'd just like to encourage you to trust in their love for you.

"Now, for the biggie, and this is a tender subject, I know, but I really need to express my feelings as Kristy's mom. She is my treasure, my beautiful little girl, no matter how grown up she gets. Her dad and I love her with every fiber of our being and we want happiness and joy for her life. We have prayed for a loving Christian mate for all our children, for over ten years, every day, we pray for them.

"It's so important that the mate she chooses has a life-long, loving commitment; that she is his treasure and he is hers, that hand-in-hand with the Lord at their side, they live a life that gives love and warmth and joy to all those around them; that they are connected in soul, heart and purpose; that they each be vulnerable to each other, see one another's faults as well as the attributes, that each one is in the other's corner, lifting them up; when disagreements arise, that they will seek a solution or compromise rather than a victory for only one; that they understand one another and seek to serve one another and communicate in a loving manner. Marriage is so important, it's a life-long commitment before God.

"It's living life with one person, loving one person forever.

"I don't see two people getting married just because they created a baby. If the love isn't there, the commitment will be shallow and the baby would be a most unfortunate child without parents who love each other.

"If you and Kristy don't love each other, don't get married. We don't want an unhappy life for either of you. There are other options. I'm not sure what they are, but if you or Kristy want our help in anything, we'll be there for you both.

"There is one more very important subject I'd like to talk about.

"Kristy is carrying a beautiful little child. It's important to her and the baby that she be at peace and surrounded by caring, loving friends and family. The physiological changes her body is going through will cause emotional trauma throughout the pregnancy. It's important that she not be exposed to undue stress. Angry words, unsolved problems, unkind remarks, friends being judgmental, all these things can cause physical damage to the baby and psychological damage to Kristy. She truly is in a very delicate condition and it's very important for you, her closest circle of friends and her roommates, to protect her emotionally.

"Sal, if there's anything I'd ask of you, as Kristy's mom, it would be to just be her friend. You don't have to marry her. You don't have to love her. You don't have to date her. You don't have to be responsible for her or the baby. You and _____ and _____ and _____ and _____ are her closest friends and share this precious secret. Kristy needs you all to resolve any personal fears you each might have as quickly as possible and not take sides or divide each other, but just be kind, caring friends.

"Loosen up, big boy, it's all going to work out 'cause Kristy, the baby and you are in God's loving hands.

"Remember you are loved,

"Lyndi McCartney

"P.S. I have to say it, I just have to. I'm deeply disappointed that you and _____ and _____ and _____ advised Kristy to kill a defenseless baby. That truly hurt my heart. Thank God each of your parents never did that to you, for the world would be a sad place without the four of you in it. I think each one of you is a terrific person."

I don't know that in my nearly fifty years on this earth I have ever read a better example of Christian love.

I thought about Lyndi's letter as I pondered exactly what I should say to Sal. I had been waiting for him to come to me, but was beginning to realize that wouldn't happen.

I had recruited Sal from his Oceanside, California hometown in 1986. Of Samoan descent, Sal was an athlete with both spirit and talent—he just needed a little practice in application. A Proposition 48 kid, Sal's high school grade point average and SAT scores prohibited him from playing football during his freshman year. But even though Sal couldn't be a contributor his first year in, the tremendous potential he'd shown on his high school team had garnered him wide-flung attention as a national recruit. I knew that, in the long run, Sal Aunese would be a major contributor to our team.

On the Colorado campus, Sal was well-liked. In his three years at Colorado, he had earned a solid reputation for his talent on the field and his loyalty to our team.

What was I going to say to Sal Aunese? In the end, I prayed that God would give me the right words.

One morning I sent word through Coach Barnett that I wanted to see Sal in my office before practice. Sal appeared in the doorway around three that afternoon. I waved him in. He closed the door as he entered, avoiding my eyes as he took a seat facing my desk. I was choked up even before I began to speak, and only with tremendous difficulty was I able to get any words out at all. But I was determined to say what was on my heart.

I cleared my throat, praying for composure. "Sal, I asked God for the right words to say to you—but I'm not at all certain I can speak them."

Sal nodded slightly, his eyes riveted to the floor.

I took a deep breath and began. "I just wanted you to know that you don't need to accept any responsibility for Kristy and the baby if you don't want to. I. . .I want you to do whatever you feel in your heart is right for you. Do you understand?"

"I understand, Coach," Sal said, shifting his gaze to the wall.

"What has happened to you and Kristy has happened. We don't want to compound the problem and make it worse. There is no animosity, only forgiveness in our hearts. You have no obligation of any kind. Whatever responsibility you want to take, we support you. If you don't want to take any responsibility, we support you there, too. Sal, I feel strongly about this: if you're not in love with Kristy, you shouldn't marry her."

I waited for a response. There was none.

I went on. "Kristy is going to be okay, and we're going to carry on, with God's help. Kristy has told us that she loves you—but that in itself isn't reason enough for you to marry her. Not unless you love her."

Sal looked up and our eyes met for the first time. I waited. Sal remained silent.

"One last thing," I added.

Sal nodded.

"Your position on this football team is not threatened."

The whole time, Sal sat in a chair across from me, most of the time staring at the floor or at the wall. He had nodded a couple of times, and once or twice said, "I understand, Coach." Outside of that, he said nothing. We were together about ten minutes, and he left for the practice field.

A few minutes later I asked Coach Barnett to speak with Sal, to assure him of my sincerity. They talked, and to this day I have never asked either what was said.

During the next six months, our lives seemed to fall into a holding pattern of some sort.

There seemed little else to do regarding the coming baby. Little else, that is, except to pray for some sort of healing—some sort of wholeness—to develop in the hearts and relationships involved. Lyndi and I continued to support Kristyn in her decision to have the baby in Boulder. Sal continued to withdraw from Kristy, dating other women on campus.

On October 15, we beat Kansas, and began gearing up for the coming game against Oklahoma. It would be a nationally televised game, and the first night game in the history of Folsom Field.

Clearly, I was feeling the pressure. Two days before the Oklahoma game, I lost my cool on the practice field.

Taming my temper was hardly a new struggle for me. As far as I'm concerned, there have been too many times when I've reacted and then regretted a burst of anger on the sidelines. And in the season of 1988, my temper continued to plague me.

I don't deny it. I was more than a little concerned about how I would react under the pressure of the meeting with Oklahoma. I prayed for victory—on the field, as well as on the sidelines as I wrestled with my temper.

On the day of the the big game, former CU athletic director Eddie Crowder came to me with a Scripture verse on anger and I loved him for it. That night, I decided to take off the headsets, thus cutting off communication with the coaches in the press box, in an effort to stem my anger.

Oklahoma got a late field goal and beat us 17-14.

I worked hard to focus my perspective away from the loss, and onto the larger priorities—the eternal matters—in life. The next day I wrote:

> Jesus, thank You for each situation, each disappointment, each setback. All of my hope is in You. I want to feed the hungry, find the lost, console the downtrodden, open my arms to the lonely. Lord, strengthen me, improve my character that I might do Your will.

The following Saturday we beat Iowa State 24-12 but I raged against one of our coaches at halftime.

I was still struggling with my temper! I read a Bible passage that said a man must deny his very self and follow Jesus. And I wrote:

> Lord, that part of me that wants to impress the world, give me victory over that. I confess I judge people harshly. Please forgive me.

On November 5, we were to play at Missouri. My old grade school, high school and college pal, Woody Widenhofer, was coaching the Tigers but was under heavy criticism. I was torn between wanting what was best for me—and wanting something good for Woody.

The night before the game, I tried to talk to Woody about Jesus Christ. I shared the Gospel the very best I knew how, and asked God to penetrate Woody's heart and reveal himself to my long-time friend.

Later that night, I wrote:

> My hopes and thoughts are really selfish. I want success for our efforts. What is Your thinking, Lord? How should I be thinking? How about Woody's job? If Missouri

winning would mean help for Woody in his job and his relationship with You, then let Missouri win.

We played an almost flawless game, beat the Tigers 45-8 and improved our record to 7-2.

You'd think that experience would have taught me something about praying unselfishly, about submitting to something other than my own will. But that's a hard lesson to learn, and the day before we left for Lincoln to play Nebraska—as my journal proves—I found myself giving in to a measure of greed. I wrote:

> Jesus, be with us as we travel. Lord, I need Your presence in all that I do. You are my strength, my joy, my life, my incentive, my fulfillment. You have the words to everlasting life. *I need You to beat Nebraska!*

We lost, 7-0. So much for selfish prayers.

On Sunday I wrote in my journal regarding the contest against Nebraska:

> Lord, thank you for my circumstances. I rejoice in knowing you control my life. Yet I am beleaguered, I am frustrated. We could have won. We have players hurt. Lord, I need your help!

I surely needed God's help, not just for my players and my staff, but for me! We were coming to the end of the season. There had been so much turmoil—on and off the field!—and I was feeling the effect.

On November 19 we beat Kansas State 56-14. That same week we received a bid to play in the Freedom Bowl at the end of December.

Early the following week, we gathered together for our team banquet. There was a "coming together," a spirit of fellowship that prevailed. Then, on Thanksgiving Day, I wrote down all the things I was thankful for, and my blessings took up an entire page!

In early December, all the coaches were out recruiting. Some of our players missed some mandatory workouts. After a lot of time in prayer, I suspended nine players. Almost immediately, I restored eight of them, provided they made up the work with extra workouts.

We weren't scheduled to play the Freedom Bowl game until December 29, still weeks away, yet I was going at a hectic pace. I was either in airplanes, hotels, a rental car; recruiting players on their turf or visiting with them as they visited the Colorado campus.

It seems that I had time for everything but patience. The day before Christmas, I came down hard on our squad. I made it plain that a first-time offence for drugs meant instant dismissal from the team. Call it tough love or whatever you wish, but I was resolved to confront every problem head on—to produce a team willing to adhere to strict rules and discipline.

On December 29, Lyndi's and my twenty-sixth wedding anniversary, we lost the Freedom Bowl game to Brigham Young. All of us were sent reeling by the defeat. It left such a sour taste with the players, the coaches and our fans. On New Year's Eve, I was so down that I wrote in my journal:

> Could it be that in one game, on one night, I have lost favor with all but you, Lord?

We had certainly lost favor with some of the nation's writers and broadcasters!

We finished twenty-fifth in the Associated Press poll. And then, in mid-February, I received word that *Sports Illustrated* was about to print two devastating articles about college football, one itemizing all the so-called ills of the game, the other pointing directly at the University of Colorado and practically accusing us of scraping the bottom of the social and academic barrel to turn our program around.

Despite the advance warning, I could never have prepared myself for the words used to describe our program and the behavior of some of our players. It discredited our entire program and left little doubt in anyone's mind that the university was willing to break, bend or bypass every rule in the book to produce a winner.

In the face of such an attack, I held on the best I could, grappling with the desire to strike back with vehemence.

Despite the controversy, recruiting went well. We didn't get all the players we wanted, but we could see a marked improvement and a gradual growth in quality as we headed into spring football drills for what would be our eighth season, and the University of Colorado's 100th season of football.

March was a roller coaster. Kristy, now eight months pregnant, felt terribly lonely and abandoned. A couple of our players had scrapes with the police. The brightest day was Lyndi's birthday, although one of our star players ruined it by threatening to leave school.

A few days later, some members of our squad called a meeting and protested that they couldn't make ends meet on scholarship. They wanted more money. Tensions ran high, yet NFL scouts who came to check out our seniors called them the most punctual, most considerate and most dependable group they'd seen. I prayed daily that I could give this group of young men the leadership required to turn them into a *team*, instead of merely a group of talented individuals.

Nearly seven months had passed since my very first journal entry—and since the tearful news of Kristyn's pregnancy. It had been a rocky season between Kristy's heartbreak, my personal war on anger, confrontations won and lost on the gridiron, *S.I.*'s searing accusations about our team. . .

But maybe we were past the worst of it.

After all, we were standing at the threshold of a fresh season, anticipating the birth of the new life Kristy had been nurturing in her body. We were several weeks into the fresh stirrings of spring. And we were going into our eighth season with the harvest of a successful recruiting campaign. It was almost possible to believe the tide had turned; that we finally had a chance to grow beyond the turmoil.

And then on March 29, it seemed the whole world came crashing down.

I was in my office when I got the news. Our trainer, Dave Burton, called and told me he'd just spoken with an oncologist in Denver. The news was devastating, but confirmed.

Sal Aunese had cancer.

He was going to die.

Three

The Dark
Before the Dawn

"They say he may not live out the week," Dave's voice came thinly over the line.

"Can they operate?" I asked, my heart in my throat.

Dave confirmed my worst fears. "It's inoperable—some radical form of stomach cancer. Very rare. And almost always fatal."

My mind raced back to an incident one month earlier, when Sal had been engaged in an off-season conditioning program and had coughed up some blood. Determined, Sal had insisted on finishing that day's workout in the field house before turning in his towel and heading for the doctor. The doctors had suspected pneumonia. But now it seemed they'd been mistaken.

I visited Sal in the hospital the following day. A couple of his teammates, David Gibbs and Okland Salavea, Sal's best friend, arrived shortly after I did. Words like devastated, crushed, hopeless—they're not nearly sufficient to describe how all of us felt. I thought of Kristy. She was so very confused and pained. How could young people possibly see the sense of all this? How could they have the wisdom and strength and faith to understand how a vibrant young life could be snuffed out in the twinkling of an eye?

For that matter, I was having a hard time accepting it all myself. I prayed fervently that God would intervene and spare Sal from death.

Most of our players were home with their families for spring break. Immediately, together with our coaching staff, I began calling around the country, trying to reach everyone with the news. Many of our athletes hurried back to Boulder to be close to Sal.

We began spring practice on April 3.

On April 4 Sal began chemotherapy.

At the same time, Kristy's doctor told her the baby was almost in position for birth.

I found myself very irritable in practice, and suspended two players for breaking rules. Later that week I went to Boulder Hospital for some counseling on how to deal with grief and how to handle bereavement.

How I wanted to do or say something to give my beautiful daughter a lift—something to encourage her, to brighten her life. She loved Sal and she knew now he did not love her. He had been seeing others before his illness became known, and now he was totally insensitive to Kristy. He had another girlfriend and Kristy was devastated. I do not hesitate to say that I was terribly angry because of the hurt Sal had inflicted on my daughter. I prayed that God would heal Kristy's feelings toward Sal, that God would heal Sal physically and spiritually, and that God would help me to sort it all out.

On April 9 our team had its first scrimmage, and Sal came and sat in the stands with members of his family who had flown in from California to be with him during his illness. Three days later Sal felt strong enough to attend class. Somehow we grabbed hold of some hope that he would be okay. I spent every spare moment in prayer.

In the book of James it says that the prayers of a righteous man can accomplish much. I could remember a recent area of my life in which I hadn't been very righteous, and wanted to reconcile anything that might keep my prayers for Sal and Kristy from being effective. On April 14 I called Rick Reilly and asked him to forgive me for the terrible things I'd harbored in my heart following his article in *Sports Illustrated*.

A few days later, my good friend Jim McFadden came from Fort Collins to pray with Kristy. Jim, now retired in Colorado, had been dean of the School of Natural Resources at the University of Michigan, and I'd met him when he was a coordinator in the Word of God Community in Ann Arbor. Jim is a great man of God, and I knew his prayers helped Kristy.

By now Kristy was nearing the end of her pregnancy. On April 20 I spoke at a Fellowship of Christian Athletes banquet—Sal and members of his family were in attendance, and I prayed that the meeting might plant some seeds of faith in Sal's heart. The next day was Kristy's due date. Three days later she still hadn't delivered, so Lyndi and I took her to a movie and to Saturday mass.

Kristy went into labor Sunday morning. On Monday the baby was born, and I wrote in my journal:

> Timothy Chase arrived 3:36 a.m., 8 pounds, 15 ounces. Thank you Father. Glory to God! A healthy mom and baby. Thanks for Sal being there.

During the day, Sal and his family came to see Kristy and the baby. On Tuesday I handed out cigars to the players. When the baby was a few days old, a priest friend—Father Bob Leib of Boulder—arranged a meeting between Kristy and Sal. The two young people met with the priest in our home. During the conversation, Sal apologized to Kristy. Kristy dared to hope that it might be the start of a new level of communication between the two of them.

We concluded our spring drills with the annual spring game on April 29. I let my hopes run away with me and schemed for 50,000 spectators to be there. I prayed, too, for protection from serious injury for our players.

I got part of what I had desired. Even though there were only 13,600 at the game, I was able to write in my journal:

> Thank you, Father. Our spring workouts were excellent. We have momentum. Our squad is healthy. There was a wonderful half time tribute to Sal, including a card, banner and the gift of a chair for him. Sal told everyone "See you next year!" We had a little party at our home after the game and the Aunese family was there.

As I went to bed that night, I knew there would be other, greater battles in the days ahead, and that my family and I surely would be scarred and tested. Yet I was able to write this last line:

> Thank you, Jesus, that I can bring everything to You in prayer.

"I don't consider myself terminally ill. I'm just a little sick."

Those were Sal's words as the month of June unfolded. He had endured two months of chemotherapy, during which time he turned twenty-one. To celebrate his birthday, he had gone back to his hometown in California where the city held a day in his honor.

While he was home, Sal had been interviewed by Terry Monahan of the *Escondido Times-Advocate*.

"Something always seems to happen to me," Sal told Monahan. He talked about how he had missed fall practice in his freshman year because of Proposition 48; how he had been suspended during spring practice of his sophomore year; and how the illness had cost him his third straight spring drill.

"Of all the bad things that have happened, the Prop 48 thing was the best thing for me," Sal admitted. "It was a slap in the face. It really woke me up. Up until that happened, I disliked school because I always had football. Then, all of a sudden, it was gone, and it was my fault. At that time I set a goal for myself to graduate from Colorado on time."

The cancer hadn't changed that goal. Sal still planned to graduate on time. In fact, he planned to take two summer school classes as soon as he returned to Boulder.

Monahan wrote of the encounter:

> When you first see Aunese, the thing that strikes you right away is the way he's handling his illness. It seems as if nothing is wrong. He has not retreated from his family and friends or even well-wishers. He still smiles a lot. Basically, he's still the same old Sal.

Except Sal Aunese was dying.

Not that anyone was ready to admit it, of course. Sal had lost eighteen pounds, then gained some of it back. That gave some of us the hope that a miracle was in the making. No one could have been more optimistic than Sal himself.

The first week of June, Sal came back to Colorado from California to get ready for summer classes and to resume treatment at University Hospital in Denver. In an unexpected turn, doctors told Sal the cancer had begun taking a heavy toll on his lungs. They decided to keep him in the hospital.

Our hopes plummeted at the news.

Mid-June I wrote in my journal:

> Kristy, Lyndi and T.C. (my grandson, Timothy Chase) visited Sal in the hospital yesterday. He has taken a turn for the worse. . .
>
> Lord, I pray for Sal, that I might have the opportunity to share You with him.

We all were hurting. And searching for some way to make sense of what was beginning to seem like an inescapable tragedy.

On two occasions I had heard Pastor James W. Ryle speak at different gatherings. I could not recall a time when a man's message had impacted me as much as his did. He was dynamic and convicting and he made me want to hear more and learn more about God's plan for my life. He challenged me as I had not been challenged since the day, years earlier, when I had asked Jesus Christ to take control of my life.

James Ryle pastored a church near our home in Boulder. Lyndi and I decided to visit his church—although with more than a little uneasiness on my part. It was the first time in my life that I planned to attend church somewhere other than the Catholic church. But I knew that God could minister to me in many settings, and I wanted to be open to His will if He had something for me to learn in a new environment.

We attended Pastor Ryle's church on June 25 and I felt more at-home there than I had anticipated. Maybe God had a reason for us to be there, after all.

Two days later, doctors told me that Sal was weakening.

I drove to the hospital the next day. As I walked the corridor toward the elevator that would take me to Sal's floor, I thought about Sal's sister Ruta. She had come from California to be at Sal's side, and was with him nearly every waking moment. And what a marvelous woman of God she is! In the past weeks, she and I had enjoyed many chats about Sal and about our faith in God. I remembered her saying that she didn't feel she should be the one to pray with Sal about salvation. She had said she felt the Lord telling her that I was the one to do it.

Moments later I opened the door to Sal's room and walked in.

Sal was not very alert that day. Remembering Ruta's words— and my own heart's desire that Sal should come to know Jesus Christ in a personal way—I brought up the subject of God. Before

I left the room, Sal and I prayed together, but somehow it was not the right time for him to make a decision to follow Jesus. He was still struggling.

That night I wrote in my journal:

> Lord, please work mightily in Sal's heart. Kristy is hurting, feeling rejected and bitter toward Sal.

Why could I not reach Sal? Why could I not put the right words together—words that would soften his heart? And where were the words to mend Kristy's hurt?

The painful fact was that Sal had sent a message to Kristy through one of our team doctors. He had said he didn't want Kristy to come around. He didn't want to see her. He only wanted to see the baby.

On July 5 I wrote in my journal:

> Lyndi called Ruta and talked with her about the chasm between Kristy and Sal. In response to Sal's message about not wanting to see Kristy, Lyndi told Ruta that Kristy and Timmy are one, and that Sal just can't separate them like that. Lord, You alone can heal this hurt.

My daughter Kristy was hurting so very much, and all Lyndi and I could do was shower her with love and understanding. Our twenty-four-year-old son, Mike, shouldered a lot of the responsibility and seemed to take on an extra burden by reaching out more than ever to Kristy and to little Timothy Chase. As a result of Kristy's ordeal, a wonderful, paternal instinct had been developing in Mike.

About that time, Lyndi wrote down some of Kristy's thoughts, gathered from conversations Kristy and Lyndi shared during those dark months. She wrote about events and feelings before and after Sal sent the message for Kristy to stay away, and Kristy has given us permission to include her thoughts in this book:

"From the beginning of June, a coolness and a tension seemed to fill the air when Timothy and I were with the Auneses. I couldn't understand it. Sal grew distant, too. He had good days and bad days. His pain grew constant. He seemed to really withdraw from most everyone. It was the first time I'd seen Sal in emotional pain, or pain that I recognized. He cried in his mother's arms; she was crying, too. It almost tore my heart out.

"There were times when I felt like an absolute outsider—and I couldn't explain why it should be that way. One day I went to the hospital with Mom and with T.C.—but I asked Mom to take the baby in to see Sal without me.

"I knew that girl—Sal's new girlfriend—was in there with him, and I just didn't want to see her. I had felt her hostility toward me before, and I felt the same way about her.

"Ruta, Sal's sister, came into the waiting room and talked with me, and after that I agreed to go in to see Sal.

"But he wouldn't even look at me. That girl was sitting next to him. She made nasty faces at me, and then laughed. What kind of stupid game was she playing? When I left Sal's room, I decided that I'd wait until someone called for me to come back and bring the baby. I wouldn't go on my own again.

"That night, after Mom and I got home after taking Timothy to the pool, I received a message by phone. The message was that Sal wanted to see his child, but not its mother! The rage within me just spilled out. I became hysterical. I hate him, I hate him, I hate him! That's all I could think of to say. I ripped his giant picture into little pieces. All I ever wanted out of life was to give Sal a reason to live, to give him as much time with his child as possible. How could he do this to me? I have no dignity, no love, no pride. I've given everything I have to him.

"I took the baby to the nursery and collapsed on the bed in pain. When I opened my eyes, it was dark. I was alone. Mom had taken Timothy and taken care of him. I don't know how long I lay there. I couldn't move, I couldn't think. I was just numb. It was morning before I could manage to stir.

"When I got up, I pulled myself together, clasped my child close to me and I thought, 'We're a team. It's you and me, kid, against the world. I won't let anyone take you away. We'll always be together. Don't you ever worry. Mommy's here, always, always, always.'

"Mom and Ruta talked over the telephone, and I heard Mom say she didn't know how much hurt I was expected to take. I didn't know how much more I *could* take. I had been there for him, given him my love, and now he was rejecting me even as a friend. My whole family was trying to pour out love to him and his family, and praying for a healing miracle.

"We'd made plans to get together with the coaches and their families at the pool for a little July 4th gathering, but it was impossible to have fun. Every time Mom and I looked at each other, we began to cry. A few days later, a letter arrived from Ruta. She explained that someone had filled Sal's head with stories about me. He was too weak to think straight.

"Now he was asking to see me and Timmy. Ruta spoke of how we ought to trust each other, and believe in each other, and how the Lord loved all of us.

"Ruta and Mom and I all talked on the telephone. Then Mom and I took the baby to see Sal. He was alone in the room. He was very depressed. Not even the presence of his child could bring him cheer. He had tubes in his chest, he was losing his hair and the color was gone from his face. I thought the end was surely near.

"I prayed that God would spare his life, and give Sal a chance to grow with his son. I understood that there was no competition for Sal Aunese. He was God's and no one else's. I love him. I love the way we were. But I understood then that it was over between us, and all I wanted was for him to get well. But whatever happened, I wanted Sal to be in God's eternal care."

Lyndi and I continued attending services at Pastor Ryle's church, and each time we went we felt more comfortable there. I was soon to be forty-nine years old and here I was, drifting away from the church of my childhood, yet knowing in my heart that I had a closer and more meaningful relationship with God. I never had the feeling I was discarding or even rejecting all that I had been taught, nor ignoring all the good that had come from being a regular and often a daily communicant. But God's message was clear. Pastor Ryle was touching my heart in a special way. I was growing as a Christian and thirsting after the knowledge that comes only from being immersed in God's word.

By then Sal was having a pretty good day, and then some bad ones.

I wrote on July 12:

Lyndi, Kristy and T.C. visited Sal and Ruta. Sal is weak and has deteriorated. Lord, be with him.

On July 20 I added:

Sal is not returning phone calls. It could be the end is in sight. Direct me, Lord, to know how to move in this delicate situation.

Ruta and I talked again about praying with Sal, encouraging him to accept Jesus Christ as his personal Savior. Once again, we agreed that I should be the one to approach him.

On July 22, I went into Sal's room and politely asked several visiting friends and athletes to leave for just a moment. I knelt down and held Sal's hand. There was no need for a lengthy discourse. Sal and I had talked before, and I knew he would understand what I was about to ask him.

I asked Sal if he had committed his life to Jesus Christ.

Sal shook his head. "I haven't done that," he admitted weakly.

"Would you like to do that, right now? Is it in your heart to turn to Christ and accept Him as Lord of your life?"

Sal looked at me. We were both crying. In just a whisper, he said, "Yes." And he smiled.

I was already kneeling beside him. It was just the two of us—and God. I prayed the sinner's prayer and Sal repeated every word with conviction, inviting Jesus Christ into his life. What a glorious moment in Sal Aunese's life and in mine, too! A few days later, I took Kristy and Timothy Chase to see Sal. I was praying every day that the hurt between them would be healed. What a gigantic struggle for these two young people, Sal hanging onto the thread of life and all of us wondering what would happen to this new life he and Kristy had brought into the world.

On Friday, August 11, the varsity reported for fall practice, less than four weeks before our opening game against Texas. Only through God's grace was I able to make any sense of all that was swirling about me. The only certainty in my heart was that I was on track spiritually.

We began practice the following Monday. Sal got out of the hospital and came by. When he showed up, the effect on the other athletes was visible. The players kept sneaking stares at Sal because he looked nothing like the man, the athlete, they had seen before.

Sal was gaunt, emaciated. His skin had taken on an ashen tone. He didn't move around much, and he wore a unit of some kind attached to his side to assist him in breathing. I had been seeing Sal regularly, so I'd seen the gradual deterioration in him, but for the players, the scene was more than a little unsettling. Despite the shock, the other athletes rallied around him, and Sal still wore his old, familiar smile.

In my life, the stresses were beginning to take a toll. I was trying to keep up with a heavy speaking schedule, concentrating on practices and trying to make sense of what was happening on a personal level, too. I fell into a period where I was tossing and turning all night. I'd wake up in a cold sweat with terrible fear of failure. The anguish was almost unbearable. I prayed for relief, for deliverance from the turmoil.

As it turned out, Pastor Ryle's sleep was disturbed, too.

On August 22, he showed up at practice and motioned that we needed to talk. I joined him at the sideline, where he proceeded to tell me that he'd had a dream. More than a dream, really. He said it was something God wanted me to know.

This is precisely the way he related it to me:

"In a dream I saw the Colorado University football team kneeling in a huddle on the playing field, with a dark cloud pressing down upon them. The situation seemed oppressive and hopeless. Then, suddenly, what seemed like the hand of God came forth and swept the cloud away with one quick, decisive and unchallenged stroke.

"A rainbow then appeared and penetrated into the center of the huddle. The players were wearing black jerseys and gold helmets, making the scene literally look like a pot of gold at the end of the rainbow. The light of the rainbow caused the gold helmets to become brilliant, having a radiant glow like pure gold under bright lights. Simultaneously, I saw what appeared to be energy moving all about the players in the huddle.

"Then I heard a voice say, 'This will be the golden season. I will remove the oppressive cloud that has been upon this team and I will fulfill promises that I have made to Bill McCartney. My power will move upon the players and My spirit will touch many of them. This will be their golden season.' I looked up to see where the voice came from and I saw spacious, clear blue skies with just enough shade clouds to block out the heat of the sun. The voice spoke again, 'I will bring this team under clear skies of wisdom, understanding and knowledge, and I will shade them from the heart of public scrutiny and criticism.'"

When Pastor Ryle told me about the dream I was nearly as apprehensive about hearing it as he was in the telling. We stood together and he spelled it all out in detail. I did nothing then except to write the details of his dream in my journal.

Reading God's word, I found in Jeremiah 29:8-9 these words:

> For thus saith the Lord of hosts, the God of Israel: Do not let your prophets and your diviners who are in your midst deceive you, nor listen to your dreams which you cause to be dreamed.
> For they prophesy falsely unto you in My name: I have not sent them, says the Lord.

But I also found this word:

> Surely the Lord God does nothing, unless He reveals His secret to His servants, the prophets. (Amos 3:7).

I believed the Bible when it promised that God would not do anything without first revealing it to his prophets. Maybe God was, indeed, revealing something to me through Pastor Ryle. But at the foundation of my reaction was a plea for understanding. In my prayers. . .in my journal. . .I repeatedly asked: "Lord, what is your wisdom for me?" I knew that, in the end, the answer to that question was the only thing that would matter.

Kristy was terribly forlorn. Lyndi and I tried to find words to say, things to do to bring her cheer. Kristy took T.C. and went out of town for a couple of days to try to assemble her thoughts.

Sometime that week, as our team was entering the final stages of preparing for our opening game against Texas, I was approached by a man as I walked to practice. I had not spoken with him before, and he has not returned to practice since that afternoon. He looked to be about sixty years old. He was trembling as he walked up to me.

"Coach," he said, "I feel very uncomfortable doing this. But Almighty God sent me here, and He gave me these three verses of Scripture to give to you."

The verses were written on three-by-five cards, and when I looked up, the man had turned and was walking away. I glanced again at the cards, but they held no particular immediate meaning for me. I stuffed them into my pocket and went on to practice.

Looking back from this point in time, I have very little doubt about one thing:

Those three cards arrived just in time to save two lives. They saved mine from a possible death penalty or life-sentence in prison. And they saved the life of the man I would surely have tried to kill.

Three days later, on August 30, *Westword*—a weekly tabloid that describes itself as Denver's "news and arts weekly"—came out with a nightmarish article that almost tore the heart out of my daughter and every other member of the McCartney family.

The cover said it all:

That Sinning Season:
CU Coach Bill McCartney keeps the faith—
and gets a grandson fathered by his star quarterback.

The smear was compounded by a terrible sacrilege: an artist depicted me on the cover, a tear tumbling down my cheek, a crown of thorns on my brow. My nail-scarred palms were grotesquely twisted, a shameful parody of the popular sculpture of "The Praying Hands." Underneath were these words:

The mortification of Bill.

Above me, grinning wickedly, were four devilish creatures in face masks. The clear inference was that my players were mocking me.

It was night time and Lyndi and I were at home when we first got a copy of the article. We were heart-broken. Devastated, shaking, we read it together. We cried, embraced and read on.

The writer recounted our team's early struggles, our failures on the field, some of our players' failures off the field, my shortcomings as a coach, and then dealt the cruelest blow imaginable. In six terrible and scathing pages, he heaped scorn and condemnation on our precious daughter, plainly suggesting she was a whore, a tramp, a slut. She was easy, he wrote, available for the pleasure of football players. This malevolence made trash of what two young people had thought was love.

The author wrote:

> Personally, McCartney has had trouble getting his Christian message across at home, too: His only daughter developed a penchant for partying with CU football players.
>
> Kristyn McCartney's youthful indiscretions weren't all that different from those of many college coeds, but they left a legacy: a bouncing, baby boy.
>
> Whose father is CU's star quarterback.
>
> Who is dying of cancer.
>
> CU administrators would like to pretend that none of this has happened. Some find the situation too embarrassing or sad. Others fear the consequences of acknowledging the real message here: That McCartney has lost the respect of his players and some are retaliating in one of the most humiliating, intensely personal ways imaginable. . .

All this, and thousands of words more. The only accuracies in the entire article were the descriptions of my priorities and goals for the team; my public stand on my relationship with Jesus Christ and the balanced comments from players who both favored my religious posture and those who thought it cornball at best and destructive at worst.

The writer quoted no one in particular, hiding the character assassination behind "one student who socialized with them" and "one player who had a platonic friendship with Kristyn" and "according to one student familiar with the relationship between Kristyn and the players" and "one friend" and "one player."

The headline on top of the article trumpeted:

CU Football Players Score!
But Coach Bill McCartney is the loser.

I cannot say how long Lyndi and I sat there, helpless. We had no answers, only questions. Had we not suffered enough? Did we not have enough turmoil? Hadn't we come through enough fires? How could we possibly endure this? Could we fight back? And if so, how? And to be sure, there was some of the "Why me, God?" within us.

We called our oldest son, Mike, who lives nearby. He said he'd be right over. We got our other sons, Tom, then twenty-three, and Marc, sixteen, out of bed. When the boys were finally gathered in our living room, I tried to prepare them for what they were about to read, telling them that the decision had already been made for our family to handle this crisis in a Godly way. Lyndi and I tried to set the tempo, so to speak.

Then we let them read the article.

Our older sons were numb. I would have understood if they had exhibited rage or threatened vengeance. But as I watched them, all I saw was stunned disbelief. By this time, it was in the early hours of the morning, and we were as beaten down as any family could get.

Yes, we all understood that among all the promises of God, there is not one that suggests life will be easy. It is not written that following Jesus Christ will eliminate every problem. We had no right to expect a trouble-free existence, and we accepted that.

But weren't we also allowed to question, to challenge, to wonder—even to doubt? After all, the Son of Man had proved that he was human as well as Lord by praying in the Garden that the cup pass from Him. And when He was in His moment of greatest agony on the cross, had He not cried out, "My God, my God, why has thou forsaken me?"

We were forsaken. Alone. Helpless.

I think it is difficult for the best of us, in times of great crisis or stress, to maintain that peace that passes all understanding. And

I'm convinced that we are not always immediately reinforced by the Scripture that reminds us to pray ". . .not as I will, but as thou wilt."

The boys were silent. Our shock and grief were tangible elements in the room. And yet the pain wasn't over yet.

We had to awaken Kristyn.

Four

A Golden Season in the Face of Death

It would be best for Kristyn to read the article at home with those who love her most. But nothing was going to lessen the trauma of the violation by much.

Kristy, sitting on the couch in her pajamas and robe, read just a small part of the article. Suddenly she began to squeal, then fell to her knees in anguish, in uncontrollable pain. It was sheer hell for her! There was nothing any of us could say or do to make it better. It was as if she had lost every shred of respect, of decency. The hurt was too personal and too deep. My precious daughter had been beaten, tortured, mocked and crucified by a deliberate campaign of vicious lies.

Somewhere in the misty hours of the early dawn, I came upon those three little cards the old man had handed me that day on the way to practice. On the cards were verses 12, 15 and 17 from II Chronicles, chapter 20:

O our God, will You not judge them? For we have no power against this great multitude that is coming against us; nor do we know what to do, but our eyes are upon You. . . .

And he said, 'Listen, all you of Judah and you inhabitants of Jerusalem, and you, King Jehosaphat! Thus says the Lord to you: Do not be afraid or dismayed because of this great multitude, for the battle is not yours, but God's. . . .

You will not need to fight in this battle. Position yourselves, stand still and see the salvation of the Lord, who is with you, Oh Judah and Jerusalem. Do not fear or be dismayed; tomorrow go out against them, for the Lord is with you.

The message could not have been plainer: God was saying, "The battle is not yours, it is mine. Just brace yourself and wait on me."

I knew then I was not to retaliate, to respond in any way to these despicable accusations, not even to attempt to defend ourselves.

The very next day, Kristy went to our team's practice. I wrote in my journal:

She showed courage. She faced the team. She said it was something she had to do. Thank you, Lord. That starts the healing.

I knew God wanted me to wait on Him. But trusting came hard, and I warred against bitterness. I began to search the Word of God with new needs. I read Psalm 27 where David concluded by saying, "Wait upon the Lord. Be of good courage, and He shall strengthen thine heart; wait, I say, on the Lord."

And the 3rd verse of the 37th Psalm: "Trust in the Lord, and do good; dwell in the land, and feed on His faithfulness."

And in the same Psalm, verse 7: "Rest in the Lord, and wait patiently for Him; Do not fret because of him who prospers in his way, because of the man who brings wicked schemes to pass."

The Psalms gave me comfort when I couldn't quite muster the level of trust I knew God wanted me to place in Him. David, after all, had made his share of mistakes, too. I mean, he was the best king and the best soldier and the best prophet and the best priest— and yet the worst backslider in the Old Testament. He had raped Bathsheba and caused her husband to be killed in battle; he had a lot of children by different wives; one of his sons raped one of his daughters; another son murdered still another of David's sons, and he had nothing but misery in his own family. But God sent a prophet to David, and David confessed his sins. And God is great on forgiveness. He cleansed David of all unrighteousness, and David is the only man in the Bible who is described as a man after God's own heart.

For everyone in our family, there was the terrible temptation to lash out. My friends urged me to sue the newspaper. Our family drew the circle tighter. The talk shows were full of controversy. We did not listen. We tried to stay close to each other and to God. I busied myself with our team, my family and the Word of God. Every member of our family knew that only with God's help could we face our tomorrows with any kind of hope that this, too, would pass.

In the first days of September, I recorded this journal entry:

>The response that we have gotten from the community has really been heart-warming—letters, calls, conversations. Kristy needs a hug.
>
>Instead of anxiously worrying about things I have no control over, I will just trust the Lord and His grace. Lyndi has shown Your spirit, Lord, through the *Westword* ordeal.

Kristy seems to be doing okay. Jesus, anoint her with Your spirit. Thank You, Lord!

As far as my journal was concerned, I hadn't written a single word about our upcoming opening game—or about football at all—since the publication of the *Westword* piece. And I certainly hadn't given much thought to Pastor Ryle's prophecy of our "golden season."

I want to claim every blessing, every gift that God can bestow upon me and my family. But it was so perplexing, whether to believe in another man's dream, regardless of the fact I feel he's truly an anointed person.

But something was about to happen to turn my attention back to the strange dream that seemed to foreshadow so many great things for our beleaguered team.

It began when we beat Texas 27-6 in our opening game.

The next day, a caption on the front page of the *Rocky Mountain News* caught my attention in a major way. Beneath a photo of Darian Hagan running against Texas, the caption said: "Buffs have a golden season debut."

Golden season. . .

There it was again.

The next day I wrote in my journal:

> Lord, I receive this as confirmation that You have chosen to bless me beyond measure. Overpower my unbelief with true faith and trust in You. Lord, thank You. Thank You for James Ryle and Your hand upon him.

The next week we beat Colorado State 45-20. Something else began to happen, as well. Often, when one of our players would make an outstanding play, he'd point to Sal Aunese in a special seating section near the press box. The message was clear: *This is for you, Sal.*

The following Tuesday, both wire service polls had Colorado in the top ten. On Wednesday, Kristy celebrated her twenty-first birthday.

The Illinois game at Boulder on September 16 would be Sal's last game with us. We had decided to dedicate the entire season to him. Sal was so weakened by that time that he could stay for just the first half. When it was time for the coin toss, our entire team took the field, saluting Sal in his private box. He returned the salute, and smiled as only Sal could.

The Illini had been ranked in the top ten but we won easily 38-7.

We were 3-0. Yet my anxieties would not leave. I heard James Dobson's radio show and he told about a Christian book dealing with anxiety and suggesting hours of Scripture study each day. I did not know how I could possibly put more hours into my day, but I vowed to try.

About that time, my mother was visiting us and Lyndi had her hands filled to overflowing, helping Kristy take care of T.C. and visiting with mom as well. For a long time I had included my mother in my prayers, asking God to give her a born-again experience.

On September 18, my journal recorded the answer to one prayer and the pressing urgency of another:

> My mom prayed to receive You, Lord. Please fill her with Your spirit. Thank You for answering that special prayer.
>
> Lord, Sal struggles. He called Kristy and they had a talk. His family has been asked to come to Denver to see him. Lord, give him Your power, Your mercy, Your glory.

I was praying harder and harder for Sal, but as I visited him each day, I could tell he was slipping away. I had given up trying to understand all the ways in which God works and instead was toiling with accepting by faith the things I do not comprehend.

On Saturday I informed our players that the outlook for Sal was grim.

Kristy and Timmy spent the day at the hospital. Although Sal didn't talk, he smiled with his eyes. Lyndi and I were there, too, and had a private moment with Sal, to tell him how much we loved him.

Sal died a few hours later.

I wrote in my journal:

> Sal died at about 8:45 last night. Kristy was in the room. Lyndi and I were in the hospital at the time. Lord, please take Sal home. Bless his family. Help us to adjust to life without him. I pray that you will give me the right words to speak to our players.

Even though I had tried to prepare our players Saturday morning, there was still disbelief. One of our athletes, Michael Pritchard, seemed to speak for many of our players when he said, "Everyone felt Sal would recover. It's something we decided to believe in, even when Coach McCartney told us Sal was struggling. We said to ourselves he'd pull through, no matter what. That's why we prayed every day, we wanted it to happen so much."

Dr. Wayne Gersoff, one of our team physicians, told me that Sal had told him near the end, "I'm hanging in there, Doc."

"He died a peaceful death," said Dr. Gersoff, "without suffering pain. He's been a tremendous inspiration for all of us. He was a tremendous warrior. He put up one of the greatest fights anyone could imagine."

Shortly before he died, Sal wrote this letter to his teammates:

"Don't be saddened that you no longer see me in the flesh, because I assure you I will always be with you in spirit. Hold me dear to your hearts as you know I do all of you. Strive only for victory each time we play, and trust in the Lord for He truly is the way!

"I love you all, go get 'em and bring home the Orange Bowl."

He had added, "He truly is the Way!"

The day Sal died was an open date on Colorado's football schedule. To me, it was as if God left it that way for him.

We held a private memorial service for members of the team on Monday, just before noon. In less than two hours there would be a public memorial service at the University's Macky Auditorium. I was scheduled as one of the speakers. I prayed for the right words to say, and the strength to speak them without faltering.

Shortly after 1:00, two thousand people filled the auditorium. They were there from every walk of life: a governor, corporation chieftains, former CU athlete Ed Reinhardt, players, staff, teachers, fans, plain folks off the street. Students—some clad in shorts, some carrying their books in back packs—stopped between classes to pay tribute to the fallen Samoan warrior.

Sal's relatives sang a traditional peace song and hymns.

Kristyn held Timothy Chase as she stood at one end of the casket. Members of Sal's family stood at her left. Little Timmy kept reaching for one of the flowers that lay on top of the casket.

Before it came my time to speak, I turned to my son Tom, on my right, and my son Mike, seated behind me, and asked them to pray that I'd be able to say the words that were in my heart. The strength came, and with it the composure not only to speak, but also to validate my daughter.

The fact that Sal Aunese was the father of my daughter's child was no real secret. Had I not handed out cigars to Sal's teammates? Lyndi and Kristy often brought the baby to practice, and afterward players would stop and talk with Kristy and cuddle Timmy. The baby wore a tee shirt with "8"—Sal's jersey number—on the back. And in July, shortly after Sal received Jesus Christ, he had told the

Oceanside Blade Citizen sports editor, Steve Schofield, about his son.

"He's big and he's wonderful," Sal had said. "I want to make sure people know the gift of life God has given me. Some people thought I was going to hide the fact I was going to be a father, but it was bad timing. I was sick when the baby was born. I know now what people mean when they say that having a son is a blessing. I really believe that. It's a gift from God, an experience you can't really describe."

This precious child had spent a lot of time at University Hospital. Sal had cradled Timmy in his arms even as he was undergoing chemotherapy treatment. Sal held Timmy on his lap while his teammates practiced. What secret?

Everything I said that afternoon is right here:

"It's wonderful to see all of you here. It's a wonderful room and it's jam-packed, just like it should be.

"Governor (Roy) Romer flew in from the Western Slope to be with us here. And I know that the Aunese family and each of us in the Colorado football family appreciate that kind of gesture.

"I was praying about what to say, early this morning. I was alone and the Lord gave me this Scripture and verses: I Thessalonians, the fourth chapter, the thirteenth and fourteenth verses—'But I do not want you to be ignorant, brethren, concerning those who have fallen asleep, lest you sorrow as others who have no hope. For if we believe that Jesus died and rose again, even so God will bring with Him those who sleep in Jesus.'

"Some six weeks ago, I knelt with Sal. I asked Sal if he had ever invited Jesus Christ to come in and take over as Lord of his life. He said he hadn't. I asked him if he wanted to. He said that he did. Sal prayed to receive Christ. I am grateful to have had the opportunity to be with Sal at that moment because at that moment there were no guarantees, physically. We'd been praying for a physical miracle but God gave him a far greater gift, you see. He restored Sal spiritually, which has everlasting ramifications.

"We had a service here earlier, at eleven o'clock, for the coaches and players and members of the athletic department, and those who were intimately involved with Sal. Each person who spoke gave a magnificent tribute to Sal.

"I'd like to take my opportunity to pay tribute to some of you.

"First, to our coaches and players.

"Perhaps not in recent history has a young man had the opportunity to allow a group of guys like yourselves to love him like you have. Sal knows of your affections. Sal saw first-hand your concern and care and love for him. You'll never have to go through life wondering if you expressed it properly or not. You touched Sal in the way that very few of us ever have the opportunity to enjoy.

"Okland [Okland Salavea, Sal's best friend, a young man of Samoan descent who lived in Sal's home town, and whom Sal helped recruit to come to Colorado], nobody's ever had a better friend than you.

Kristyn McCartney:

Sal was gasping for every breath —he was in so much pain. Early in the day he took off his oxygen mask and smiled and waved at T.C. He was glad that Timothy was there. All any of us could do was look at him and try not to break down. It was obvious that things didn't look good for Sal. But most of us believed he would make it through this too. The day was very sad but also was filled with a lot of love for Sal. His family and friends stood by his side, filling his hospital room, and sang some songs. He spent the day saying goodbye to everyone—in his own way. When he passed away, everyone stood at his bedside weeping and questioning why. We all just stared at him, hoping he would wake up. But he couldn't.

Sal was so lucky. You are the ultimate friend, loyal, loyal, loyal. I've never seen love like that.

"Coach Barnett [Gary Barnett, Sal's position coach], you know, in coaching, you don't always have the perfect chemistry. You don't always have the bond you want. You're always reaching for it, both player and coach, but you had it. You had Sal's respect, his trust, you were his confidant. You were his friend. It was wonderful what you and Sal had.

"Sal did one thing every football player in the country wanted to do. He was the starting quarterback on his football team and he never went through spring drills.

"Dave Burton [director of the sports medicine program at CU] and Dr. Wayne Gersoff [one of CU's team physicians], you were wonderful. You were there throughout this whole ordeal. Kept us all informed, told us what we needed to know. Gave us enough information that we could carry on, but not so much that we couldn't carry it.

"Dr. Bill Robinson [the oncologist who treated Sal at Denver's University Hospital], Sal and his family felt like they had the greatest cancer expert available.

"To our president, Dr. Gordon Gee and our athletic director, Bill Marolt, it's been a family affair.

"To the Aunese family, you have indelibly imprinted on our hearts here in Boulder and the Colorado football family, inescapably, what real family is. The love that you had, the honor that you all have shown up with, the Samoan tradition and culture, we've been so blessed. We would never have gotten to know you all like we have if we hadn't had this day. We'll never forget you.

"And Ruta [Sal's sister], Ruta, you're the superstar in all this. You have such natural strength. You are truly a woman of God. Oh, if all of us could have the opportunity to pass away with you at our side.

"Kristy McCartney, you've been a trouper. You could have had an abortion, gone away and had the baby someplace else to avoid the shame. But you didn't. You stayed here. You're gonna raise that little guy, and all of us are gonna have the opportunity to watch him. It looks like we've got another lefthander coming up in the ranks. Kristy, I admire you. I respect you. I love you so much."

I could not have anticipated that what I had to say would be a national story; no clue that what I uttered would touch girls and women all over America. Many of them have written to me. There are so many of them who have gone through similar trouble, and their fathers did not stand by them, and their mothers felt they had disgraced the family, and the father of the child walked away from it all with a shrug.

Some of the women I've heard from have undergone abortions; some have given birth to their babies; some of them have been making their decisions just as they wrote the letter, and were perplexed about what to do. I've heard from older women who went through all that awful pain years before.

The Lord used that day to minister to women as well as to validate my daughter. He reinforced her, and used that whole turbulent affair to remind me that being a Christian never means the absence of pain. And it reinforced within me that Christians have available for full-time use a sovereign, holy, mighty, wondrous, righteous God who loves us and who allows us to love the unlovely and who will give us peace when there is no peace to be found.

That afternoon, God resurrected in me a fierce spirit that commands me to tell others about Him, no matter how many crosses He lays on me.

A university psychologist was summoned to deal with some of our players who felt terrible despair over Sal's death. Grief heals slowly, and not only our players were affected, but a much larger community of people who had known and loved Sal Aunese.

One of our linemen, Bill Coleman, said at Sal's memorial

service: "We know that for us to feel sorry for ourselves or to feel sorry for his loss, well, that would disgrace Sal."

Safety Tim James: "Sal wasn't the type to quit. We've got a good thing going and we're not about to give up now."

Dick Conner, *Denver Post:* "Aunese may be impossible to dismiss. His impact as a person, a leader, a battler may go far past any he might have had merely as a football player."

His sister, Ruta: "Spiritually, there is nothing to be saddened about. This is a day of celebration, this is a day of happiness because Sal has gone home to be with the King."

Sal's high school coach, Dick Haines: "He was a great player, a great leader and a great young man. He was just a good person, a real positive person. He always had a smile on his face, and he had an inner confidence that rubbed off on everyone on the team, everyone around him."

Athletic Director Bill Marolt: "He was the one who brought vitality to the program when we needed him most."

Mike Barry, offensive line coach: "What's inconsequential now is personal glory. The season is for the glory of the team and the glory of Sal. It intensifies the quest."

University President E. Gordon Gee: "Such a spirit does not die. That spirit is now passed to us, and if we have the character and commitment to pick up the torch, Sal Aunese will be a part of us all."

I credit our players for the way they rallied, winning at Washington the Saturday after Sal died. We enjoyed a great victory that day over the Huskies.

A group of us traveled to California on Monday to pay tribute to Sal. We joined Kristy and T.C. who had been there since Friday.

There were three hundred mourners at Sal's funeral in Vista. "Sal touched us unlike any player has ever touched a college football program or a community. When we won, Sal deflected the praise to his teammates. When we lost, he took the blame."

I told that to Sal's friends and family gathered there, and they knew the young man as I had.

Meanwhile, back home in Colorado, mail was pouring in over the things I had said at Sal's memorial service.

Two days later, we beat Missouri, my alma mater, 49-3. We filled Folsom Field.

Kristy flew with us on the team plane for the game at Ames, Iowa. The good news is that we defeated Iowa State 52-17. The bad news is that our leading ground gainer, Eric Bieniemy, broke his leg. Still, expectation among Colorado fans was at fever pitch.

We kept moving up in the national polls. On October 21, Kansas succumbed 49-17.

USA Today interviewed me four days later. I wrote in my journal that I felt a little uneasy sharing my spiritual perspective with

Bill Curry, head football coach at Kentucky and a man of strong Christian principles:

I've got a daughter the same age as Kristyn McCartney, and ironically, her name also is Kristin. When I think about what Bill McCartney has had to endure, and then how he led Sal Aunese to Christ, I am totally overwhelmed. That's as far as it goes, that's as strong as it gets. When he faced the ultimate test—not as a coach but as the father to the daughter he loves more than life itself—he responded by givng the ultimate gift.

non-believers, even though my heart wanted very much to proclaim publicly my faith in God. I asked God to direct me in these
interviews; to help me get rid of the uneasiness I always felt.

Next was Oklahoma—at Norman, Oklahoma. We had lost the
last twelve games to the Sooners, and had not won a contest on
their turf since 1965. I experienced great edginess, seeing our obvious weaknesses, pondering Oklahoma's great strengths. I prayed
for a calm spirit, for wisdom.

Our defense played superbly. We won the game 20-3.

About that time, I allowed myself to fantasize about a perfect
season, a Big Eight championship. I worried that I was being vain;
that I lacked humility. But the fact was that we were now 8-0. The
season was turning into an unprecedented coup for our beleaguered team. And each time we won, another shadow of doubt
was cast away and the words of Pastor Ryle were thrust farther into
the forefront of my thoughts: *This will be their golden season. . .*

If anything had the potential of bringing my hopes back down
to earth, it was the fact that we were scheduled to play Oklahoma
and Nebraska back to back—our record against Nebraska was even
less promising than our record had been against Oklahoma.

Yet somehow, the week between the two games was exciting,
and anticipation ran high. I remember mentally gearing up not
only for the game, but for an anti-abortion rally with Operation Rescue. I was slated to speak at the rally just days after
our contest against Nebraska.

On Saturday we played Nebraska. And we won: 27-21. It was
the first time in sixty-six years that Colorado had a 9-0 season start!

It was also the first time I felt the full wrath of the nation's
pro-choicers.

As Lyndi and I approached the pro-life rally where I was scheduled to speak, hordes of protesters waited for us outside. Lyndi
was anxious, but I was excited about another chance to
proclaim my faith.

Within days, the editorials in Colorado papers were stocked
with letters spouting angry words about my public stand on

abortion. More pointedly, anonymous letters began showing up in my mail: "Stick to coaching, you idiot! Stay out of things that are none of your business!" . . . "Leave the politics to the courts! You have your hands full getting ready for Oklahoma State!"

Everyone had advice for me. Well-meaning Christians sent me verses of Scripture, purporting to illustrate how terribly sinful I was being by taking such a public stand. All I did was pray about it. And I came away more convinced than ever that God was telling me to speak out.

On Saturday, we gained another great victory on the field. After falling behind by 10 points in the contest against Oklahoma State, we rallied for 41 points—and won the game 41-17. Our team was hailed for its 10-0 record. I, on the other hand, was vilified for railing against the killing of unborn children.

Suddenly, the tide of

Bo Schembechler:

Over a long career in coaching, I've had some turbulence with the media. You only learn to deal with the media, I think, after you get some experience and maybe only after you've been burned a few times. I think you always have to be perfectly honest, but that's not to say that you have to bring up material they don't task for.

There's a way to be fair without telling everything you know. You don't have to empty your mind, you know! Last year, when he beat Nebraska, I called Bill to tell him how proud of him I was. Right away he started telling me how the press was killing him, just eating him alive, because he'd taken such a strong public stance on the abortion issue. "They're just eating me alive," he said.

Then he told me he had

(Continued)

public outcry turned. There began an outpouring of support for the stand I had taken against abortion. By midweek following the Oklahoma victory, I was getting fifty to sixty supportive letters every day.

The morning of our final regular season game against Kansas State, I wrote in my journal that I was not taking KSU for granted, and that I hoped our players wouldn't, either. They didn't. We won the game 59-11.

Five days later, Dick Connor wrote in the *Denver Post* that it was a lot easier just to accept Bill McCartney than to explain me.

That next weekend, Miami beat Notre Dame 27-10.

The University of Colorado Buffaloes became the number one college football team in the nation. We would play Notre Dame in the Orange Bowl on New Year's night. There would be one more poll after that.

But first, it was time to let go and relax for just a bit. I played nine holes of golf and played such a lousy game that I spent just a tiny bit of time in prayer asking God if there wasn't a little something He could do about that.

But for the most part, relaxing meant spending time with my family, enjoying the great blessing we had in T.C.—and, of course, doing some reflecting on the months that had brought us to this place in time. There had been inconceivable pain and unprecedented glory. . .

. . .and God's hand had somehow stayed locked in control in the worst and best of times.

I was sure of that now—a lot surer than I'd felt months ago when I first learned of Sal's cancer, wept through the *Westword* ordeal, or even listened, perplexed, to Pastor Ryle's prophetic dream.

They say hindsight is 20/20. Looking back farther now, through the years that culminated in our Golden Season, it's possible to see how God was hard at work on a more full-time basis than I typically gave Him credit for at the time.

I think that when you've just come through the mountains and valleys of triumph and despair—like we had—you tend to ponder these sorts of things.

You think about the human element, as well. You remember the individuals who invested themselves in your life; some of them to the point that every triumph in your life is a tribute, in a very real sense, to them as well.

consented to speak at a pro-life rally that next week, and I couldn't believe my ears. "For crying out loud, Bill, that could have waited until the season was over. This isn't the time for that!"

There was a little pause, and finally he said, "Bo, the Lord told me to do it."

And then I paused. I just said, "Oh." If the Lord told Bill McCartney to do it, then Bo Schembechler certainly didn't have any further questions.

But Bill's the kind of guy who's so forthcoming that if you ask him for the time of day, he'll tell you how to make a watch. I know that in my own case, there were some things I learned only through maturity, and one of them was not to volunteer too much information. Once you've been through the swamp a time or two, you learn where the alligators are hanging out and you just have to avoid them.

Five

Tough Lessons Learned Well

He was Irish, Catholic, Democrat, Marine and blue collar. He's dead now, but I don't know that even now, with the advantage of hindsight and the clarity that retrospection is supposed to create, that I could break it all down and determine which of those things was most important to him.

He was William Patrick McCartney and he was my father. He was a remarkable man, too generous to lie, too brave to cheat, an extremely loyal human being and one of the most intense people I've ever known. In a sense, he has been my biggest fan, and I his.

He was born at the turn of the century and was white-haired by the time he was twenty. I suppose you'd have to say his world was pretty small; he didn't travel much—just to work, to church and to athletic contests. Those things, and his religion and his family, they were his life.

My mother and he brought three sons into the world. She'd

had a daughter by a previous marriage but Jeanine, a teenager by the time I arrived on August 22, 1940, didn't live with us. She married at seventeen and moved out when I was very young. Between the two of them, my mom and dad gave me and my brothers everything that was really important in life.

We were given to understand right away that a fancy house, fast cars and dollars in our pockets were not the really important things in life. Tom, two years older than I, and Richard, nine years my junior—got the same lessons I did. They were good lessons, sometimes learned tough but learned well. And when we were a little slow in the learning process, the old man had a way of dealing with that, too.

My mother, Ruth Lloyd McCartney, was a wonderful mother and I'd have to say pretty much a subservient wife. It seems she lived just to please my father, and to make life as nice as possible for the children. My father worked for Chrysler Corporation and had helped make the old De Soto cars. He was already forty-one when I was born, so all his opinions had already been formed and no smart-aleck kid was about to change any of them.

I grew up believing a lot of those things: That Notre Dame was the greatest university on the face of the earth, and that Catholics were the only people who'd be in Heaven.

Bill McCartney

We lived in a two-bedroom house just across the street and down three houses from Riverview High School, in a downriver section of Greater Detroit where ninety percent of the people who worked got dirt and grime under their fingernails while doing it. The old man had the respect of his fellow workers, and each year they'd elect him to be one of their officials. For twenty straight years he was secretary-treasurer of his union local, and I remember him sweating out the election each year, wondering if the guys would put him back in office. But every year they did.

Early on, he made us understand what was important to him:

He was fiercely proud of his Irish heritage and it didn't take much to get him to brag about it; voting for Democrats was important because that was the party of the working man—the people who cared about the little people; Catholicism was critical simply because that's what God intended for you to do with your spiritual life; the Marines taught him to be tough, and as for hard work, that was simply what was expected of every good, red-blooded American.

When I played basketball and football at Riverview High, he'd be in the stands, on his feet when things weren't going well, leading the student body in this cheer: "One, two, three—kill the referee! Three, two, one—kill the other one!"

At halftime, he'd position himself so the referees would have to walk right by him on their way to their dressing room, and he'd say, "You know, I used to think you were one of the best officials in the whole downriver area, but this is about as bad as I've seen you tonight."

He'd do anything he could—including calling the officials "Jesse James"—if he thought his team was getting robbed.

No shrinking violent, this old Marine!

He had won his Purple Heart, so wounding the feelings of some guy in a striped shirt had no effect on him at all!

Because my mother had been divorced, she really didn't participate in the Catholic Church—but William Patrick McCartney was staunch in his conviction that our family worship together. Each Sunday, the lot of us traipsed to the neighboring town of Trenton to attend mass where no one knew much, if anything, about Mom's previous marriage.

We were poor but proud. No, let me take that back. We really weren't poor, because we had a roof over our heads and three square meals a day. But we were a family of meager means, with no luxuries. And whatever my dad said, that was law. He told the same jokes over and over again, and my mother would laugh every time. She didn't jump when he snapped his fingers—not at all! She was so in tune to his needs that he didn't need to do any finger-snapping. She was just there for him, and for all us us, all the time. In today's society, that probably wouldn't work very well in most households, but back then, that was our culture. That's just the way things were.

He was such a fanatic about the Democratic Party and Catholicism that he'd become furious when anyone would condemn President Roosevelt and say he got us into World War II. And my, how my dad adored Notre Dame.

I remember once—and I couldn't have been more than seven or eight years old—my brother Tom and I sat with him in his new car in the driveway by the house, listening to a Notre Dame football game. We didn't have a radio in the house that worked all that well. When Notre Dame got a 15-yard penalty, he'd fly off the hook and start berating the officials.

"Those West Coast officials just love to give it to Notre Dame," he'd bellow.

I grew up believing a lot of those things: That Notre Dame was the greatest university on the face of the earth, and that Catholics were the only people who'd be in Heaven. And in my young heart, I just knew the United States Marines had saved the Republic with the Army and Navy merely operating in the background.

When my brother Tom—who also has had a tremendous impact on my life—got out of high school he went right into the Marines and I'm sure it was because he knew it would please Pop. Growing up, of course, Tom was always bigger, stronger and tougher than I and we got in our share of scraps—but as soon as he got into the Marines he wrote me lots of letters and encouraged and supported me. Those letters helped draw us together.

Later, when Tom got out of the service, he and I went into college at the same time. Rich probably had more pure athletic ability than either Tom or I—but he was always running into injury problems. He was an excellent student, however, and both my brothers have done really well and are very productive, very decent human beings and I love them very much.

My dad and I had two major confrontations in my early years. I guess there was one minor one, where he turned me upside down and gave me a terrific spanking even though I was a big kid all of fifteen. I had talked back to him—but when he turned me upside down and laid it on me, I stopped talking! He was, after all, six-one and weighed 195 pounds.

Our first major difficulty came when I was about fourteen, when I was certain—for the first and only time in my life—that I knew more than my dad did. Just about the time I got pretty heavily into my cocky mode, he got very heavily into his silent mode.

He simply froze me out. We didn't speak for six weeks.

Finally, it not only dawned on me that I didn't have all the answers—but I felt so doggoned terrible! I just couldn't stand the silence any longer. When I showed the proper remorse and respect, things quickly

---

Woody Widenhofer and Bill McCartney attended parochial school together, both played football at Missouri, both went into coaching. Widenhofer was on Chuck Noll's staff with the Pittsburgh Steelers, then served as head coach at the University of Missouri, and now is an assistant coach with the Detroit Lions:

Bill's a couple years older, but we were together a lot as kids because of our love of football. Bill never was a follower, even as a kid. When we'd choose up sides, Bill was the one with the natural leadership, the one drawing up the plays in the dirt.

I know they got on him a lot at Colorado, saying he recruited altar boys. But Bill was the altar boy-type as a kid. He was always very religious and more serious than the rest of us. I knew his father real well. He stayed right on those kids and made them toe the line.

(Continued)

I remember the first time I had too much to drink. I didn't dare go home, that's for sure, so I wound up staying at Bill's house, in the basement. I got sick as a dog, and Bill fed me sauerkraut. He said it'd bring me around. It finally did, but I don't know which was worse: the affliction or the cure.

Bill went to Missouri then recruited me to go there, too. Bill was a bit of a hell-raiser in college, but not as bad as the rest of the guys. He was always more reserved, a little shy—in fact, very shy—with the girls. He was always a one-woman guy. We always went to church and communion before every game, being raised Catholic like we were. It was always very important to Bill.

When we'd come home in the summer, a guy named Henry Garcia would give us construction jobs. We were rock-busters. We'd work like hell all day, then we'd stop for a beer.

One night we were supposed to meet our old high school coaches, Bud McCourt and Ernie Mayoros, to play pinochle. We had a couple of cold ones, then got in the car. About then, a carload of sailors from the Grosse Ile Naval Training Station drove by and we exchanged a few insults. Before you know it, we're out of the car and in one terrific fight.

Bill and I won the fight, but the Trenton police came and threw us in jail. When they told us we could make one phone call, we called our old coaches and they came and sprung us. They didn't think the whole thing was too funny.

Since college, we haven't seen that much of each other, but we've stayed close like old friends ought to. If he went to war, I'd be there for him, and I know he'd do the same for me. It's a matter of enduring respect.

got back to normal. As I look back on it, silence was my dad's best strategy. I could have learned a thing or two: Too often in my adult life I've met trouble head on, then realized later I would have been much better off to maintain my silence than to vent my anger and frustration. I guess—as is the case with most children, regardless of their age—we frequently are slow to acquire our wisdom.

My introduction to drinking occurred at the end of my senior year at Riverview High School. It was 1958, and my senior class had saved for four years to make this ambitious and wonderful trip to New York City. There were sixty-five kids in our class, and a group of the guys got together in a hotel room and drank beer. It didn't take much to get us silly and we weren't slick enough to conceal the evidence, so we got nailed. I don't think the term "permissive society" had been coined then, so our little escapade cast a cloud over the entire trip.

The word was out even before we got back to Riverview. And just in case anybody missed hearing it, the school administration sent letters to the parents of the boys.

It was fairly chilly around our place for quite a long spell.

And for years after that—I guess pretty much up until he died at the age of eighty-seven—whenever he'd get an audience or whenever he felt I might need to be taken down a notch, my dad would tell the story about the two vastly different letters he had received about me from the folks at Riverview High School. The first one, during my junior year, explained that I had been selected to serve on an honor court for the graduating seniors because I was in the top ten academically. It was a glowing letter, indeed, confirming that all his best hopes for me were surely being realized. Then he'd go into great detail about the second letter, the one about the drinking spree in New York. And I'd cringe every time he told it.

It was tough, watching him endure his last years. I'd always remembered him as being strong, Gibralter-like—so robust and full of life. Then he fell and hurt himself, and he wasn't the same after that.

At the very end, he wasn't himself at all, and I couldn't say all the things I wanted to say to him. Even though there was no need for any sort of death-bed reconciliation—he knew I loved him and I had expressed that to him pretty much throughout our lives together—I still wanted to sit down and kind of recap all the things he had meant to me.

He had been proud of me; he'd seen me become a college coach and have a little taste of success. But all through the years, he had been full of advice, which sometimes I took and sometimes I didn't. He had always told me that above all else, I should tell the truth, and that if I did that, nothing else would really matter. He had repeated over and over again that if a man is open and honest—and doesn't have skeletons rattling around in his closet—well, a man could derive a lot of strength from that when things weren't going well and the world seemed to turn against him, as it sometimes does.

He was authentic, the genuine article. I just wanted to look him in the eye and say, "Dad, I've been around a little bit now, and I've seen something of this world and the people in it—and I have a much greater appreciation for you, and I want you to know that I will always be grateful for the direction and guidance you gave me."

All I wanted was to have the chance to say that in person, and have him tell me that he understood.

Six

A Legacy of Champions

When I was fortunate enough to get all those coach-of-the-year honors after the 1989 season, I immediately called two people: Tony Versaci and Bo Schembechler.

Everyone has heard of Bo—he's done it all, and done it better than most folks for a long number of years. And when I told him how much I appreciated all he had done for me, and tried to articulate how much of my good fortune I owe to him, Bo, at first, tried to shut me off with a kind of "Aw, forget all the mushy stuff" comment. But I made him listen for a change, and told him I'd never forget his kindnesses, how he helped me get the head coaching job at Colorado, how much I had learned from being a member of his staff. He paused a few seconds and said, "You know, when a man gets to be sixty years old, stuff like that is kind of nice to hear."

Tony Versaci? His is not a household name but he has been

every bit as important to my career, and to my development as a coach, as has Glenn E. (Bo) Schembechler of Michigan.

For eleven years, Tony Versaci was the head football coach at Dearborn Divine Child High School. He was light years ahead of other coaches, I feel, and far and away the best high school coach in the state. And his teams were almost unbeatable. Each year in the spring, he would spend a week with Bear Bryant in Alabama. At that time, football in the South was the pacesetter. The South had the newest ideas and techniques. Coaches in the South were innovative, so Tony Versaci would come back to Michigan with his playbook and his head crammed full of the kind of information that put him well ahead of other coaches and teams in the Midwest.

When the opportunity came for me to work on Tony's staff, I jumped at it. I'd figured out a long time before that the best way to get ahead—and to get smarter—was to hang around bright people and listen to what they had to say. Plainly put, I was determined to climb the coaching ladder, and Versaci could help me.

From the time I was eight or nine years old, all I ever wanted to do was coach football.

When I was in elementary school, we'd go into the street and play touch football—and I always called the plays for guys older than I was. I seemed to have a knack for it, a grasp of what was taking place in the game. Later, I learned a lot from my high school coaches; Ernie Mayoros and Bud McCourt, my football coaches, had a tremendous impact on me.

When Dan Devine recruited me to play football at University of Missouri—I was in his first recruiting class—my instincts were a whole lot better than my ability. I played linebacker and center, but I was just a decent player, certainly not a gifted one.

At Missouri, about sixty, maybe eighty football players took a class called Theory of Football. When it came time to be tested, we analyzed what the University of Missouri was doing right and wrong in football, and I tested third behind two quarterbacks. I could just conceptually understand what was happening better than the average guy. The idea, the concept, the preparation—all the intangible things associated with football—excited me perhaps more than the mere playing of the game. I was immersed in theory, totally captivated with coaching.

After college, I stayed on for a year as a graduate assistant. I did some coaching in Missouri high schools, and then I got the opportunity to teach and coach in the Greater Detroit area where I'd grown up. Lyndi and I were married by then, and moving to Detroit would mean she would have to leave behind family and friends—but coaches rarely consider anything but career when they think they might be climbing the professional ladder. We got the job offer one day; packed and moved the next.

While teaching third grade in Taylor, a suburb west of Detroit, I became head basketball coach at Holy Redeemer High School. Holy Redeemer was a school rich in basketball

Dan Devine was one of the most successful football coaches in all of college football. He coached at Arizona State from 1955-57 and at Missouri 1958-70. He coached the Green Bay Packers from 1971-74 and the Notre Dame Fighting Irish from 1975-80. He recruited Bill McCartney to play center-linebacker in two-way football at Missouri. Said Devine:

Bill was always very serious about the game. He was not possessed with great natural ability but he more than made up for it with marvelous instincts, a mind for the game and wonderful dedication. I guess he had his moments of raising Cain, as most college students do, but he was a tough kid and a team man through and through, always on time for meetings, always eligible. He had those intangibles that make a coach's job easier.

(Continued)

McCartney helped take our team to two straight Orange Bowl games. We lost the first one, and I recall that after the game I got on some of the players—McCartney included—because I felt they had sort of lost their concentration and maybe they had violated curfew before the game. I was very tense in those days—very uptight about smoking, drinking, late hours. Too rigid, maybe.

The following year we played Navy. That year the Midshipmen had Joe Bellino, who'd just won the Hiesman Trophy as the best running back in the land. McCartney played a fantastic game against Navy that day. As a matter of fact, our entire defense did and if memory serves me correctly, we held Bellino to minus yardage on the ground and it sort of made up for our failure the previous year. [Devine's memory is flawless: Bellino had minus eight yards in twelve carries.]

Actually, that was a remarkable group of kids we had at Missouri back then. Andy Russell was on that team, too, and what a terrific player and genius of a fellow he is! Some of these men said later that we polished and nurtured them, but I think—perhaps without knowing it at the time—that we did a very good job of selective recruiting. I've always believed that if you recruit good kids, they'll win for you.

That team lost only one game—we lost our final game of the season to Kansas. We had just beaten Oklahoma 41-19 in a super emotional victory, and I wasn't smart enough—or perhaps not experienced enough—to get the players back down to earth for the game the following week. People have said, "Kansas? How could you lose to Kansas?" But in that period of time, Kansas probably had more good football players and fewer good teams than anyone in the country. Just think of players like John Hadl, Bert Coan, Gayle Sayers, John Riggins, and the list goes on and on.

We won the Orange Bowl game that year, and it was the first bowl game Missouri had ever won. Minnesota, which had been ranked number one, lost to UCLA in the Rose Bowl and I've always felt that had there been a post-bowl vote—back then the voting was done right after the regular season— that Bill McCartney's team would have been crowned the national champion.

Down through the years, Bill and I have kept in touch. When I was coaching at Notre Dame and he was defensive coordinator at Michigan, we beat Michigan two years in a row on the last play of the game. Once, we blocked a field goal attempt that would have won the game for Michgan, and the next year one of our kids kicked a winning field goal on the last play.

A few days after that second game, I was back in South Bend and received a beautiful hand-written letter from Bill. He congratulated me and our staff and team, then at the end of his letter he cautioned me: "Don't forget to give all the honor and glory to God." And I knew it was from his heart.

Some years later, when his Colorado team beat Nebraska for the first time in years, I sent him a little note and reminded him to do the same thing.

Quick as a flash, here came another hand-written note from Bill and, again, he expressed his beliefs so eloquently that it made my wife, Jo, cry just to read it.

But that's Bill. I regret to say that all too few coaches are that up-front and deep-thinking. McCartney is the genuine article.

tradition, and had recently won the state Class B Championship—so when I took over, there was a lot of pressure on me to perform well. At the same time, I saw an opportunity to work as an assistant football coach under Versaci at Dearborn Divine Child.

I was twenty-three and constantly on the go. I'd race around to wherever Adolph Rupp of Kentucky was doing a clinic and absorb everything I could about Kentucky's offense; then I'd listen to Bobby Knight of Indiana at another clinic and I became a disciple of Knight's defense. I ran Rupp's offense and Knight's defense and myself ragged.

Up early in the morning, I'd drive around and pick up some of my players and take them to basketball practice at six o clock in the morning. After practice, I'd drive furiously to Taylor to teach my third graders. Once school let out, I'd drive to Dearborn to work for Versaci and the Divine Child football team. In the evening, it was basketball practice all over again.

When I wasn't coaching ball, I was talking ball over a beer with my buddies in a saloon. I have to confess: I was not an attentive husband and father back then. I loved Lyndi and our children, but in all honesty, they had to take a back seat to my ambitions.

And football was where I really wanted to be.

The first year I was on Tony's staff, we won big. In the Catholic League championship game at University of Detroit Stadium, Gary Danielson (later to star at Purdue and in the National Football League) was 24 out of 27 for something in excess of 300 yards passing. I mean, he just cut the other team's defense to pieces.

In two years under Tony Versaci, I absorbed as much as I could. Meantime, my Holy Redeemer basketball team had won the Catholic League Championship. Then Tony got a job on the Michigan State staff under Duffy Daugherty and, at his urging, Divine Child named me athletic director, head football, head basketball coach and dean of discipline for the school!

Life could not have been sweeter! I had a beautiful and loving wife, three delightful little children, and on top of that, I thought I was a really good Christian! After all, I went to mass every day, I said my prayers, and I tried to live by the Golden Rule.

What I really had was a tiny taste of success and a tiny taste of religion—but not much Christianity. Sure, I was a good person. I treated others with respect. But someone once described the contrast between a good life and a godly life as the difference between the top of the ocean and the bottom. On top, sometimes it's like glass—serene and calm—and other times it's raging and stormy. But hundreds of fathoms below, it is beautiful and consistent, always calm, always peaceful. Down deep in my heart, I did not have the peace that comes only from knowing Jesus Christ as a personal savior. Back then in 1970, when I was twenty-nine years old and a head football coach for the first time in my life, I was a church-goer and a professing Christian. But it wasn't until four years later, when I was a rookie assistant coach at the University of Michigan that I discovered a real relationship with Jesus Christ. And when I accepted Christ as Savior and Lord of my life, I began an adventure that has transformed my life.

Nevertheless, at Divine Child, I attacked my new assignments with renewed vigor and enthusiasm.

At that time, there were sixteen junior high schools that weren't affiliated with any particular high school, meaning that students were able to choose their high school. The obvious choices for Catholic students were Bishop Borgess, Catholic Central, University of Detroit High, Sacred Heart of Dearborn. . .or Divine Child. I made up my mind that no coach would know these young players any better that I would—and I began to scout every one of them. I watched all of them play; got to know every top eighth grader and tried to convince the strong players to come to Divine Child. Many of them did. And we were able to continue the tradition that Tony Versaci had built.

Divine Child was, for one, the place where I learned how to recruit. But there was still much to learn. . .

An old pal of mind from my younger days in the downriver sector of Detroit, George Mans, had been a fine player at Michigan and had gone on to be an assistant coach for the Wolverines. Schembechler hadn't been there very long, but he was already successful, so I talked George into spending some time with me and letting me absorb the Michigan system. I recognized that if I went to Ann Arbor and used Michigan's resources, watched practices, viewed film. . .I'd be a better coach. Before long I had Bo's film, Bo's playbook, Bo's system; I even used the same terminology.

What so many high school coaches don't seem to realize is that when you avail yourself of all the good things you can pick up from college ball, it's a tremendous advantage. And I was looking for every break I could get. Good kids and a good, sound system. I knew those to be the ingredients of success.

And our program was successful right from the start. When the University of Houston installed the veer offense and knocked the socks off everybody's defenses, I hurried there and spent time with Billy Willingham, who at that time was offensive line coach under Bill Yeoman. When I installed the veer at Divine Child, our team won all nine games and captured the mythical state Class B Championship. In the same year, we also won the state basketball championship and I've been told that I'm the only coach in the history of the state of Michigan to win state championships in both football and basketball in the same school year.

I remember telling the people at Divine Child when they gave me both head coaching jobs that it was my goal to win state championships in both sports. In fact, I said as much at a Men's Club meeting and one guy there responded, "You know, Coach, we don't expect that."

And I told him, "You don't understand—that's *exactly* what we're talking about here."

Nothing would stand in my way. Not Lyndi. Not my children. Not anything. Our son Michael had been born in the fall of 1964. Tom had come along a year and three months later. A little more than four years later we had been blessed with Kristy, and by 1972

Marc—born exactly eight years after Mike—had completed our family.

In those years, Lyndi was abused. Not the physical kind of abuse, but the kind that's insidious. I was an athletic director, football coach, basketball coach and I was teaching physical education. I simply did not have the time—no, correct that: I did not *take* the time—to be the husband and father I could and should have been.

The fact is, I really can't take credit for the fine way our kids have turned out. Lyndi is the one who has been the solid rock of the McCartney family life.

When I first began coaching at Divine Child, the older boys were just little tykes in elementary school, and when they'd get out in the afternoon they'd come racing down to the gymnasium and stay through practice. When I'd get the players around me in the huddle to impart some wonderful coaching wisdom, I'd look down and there my little guys would be, crawling on

---

Lyndi Taussig McCartney was born in Oklahoma, grew up in California, and attended Stephens College, located on the University of Missouri campus, where she met her husband-to-be:

Woody Widenhofer was a football player at Missouri (later he would coach at his alma mater and is now an assistant coach with the Detroit Lions). He was also a good buddy of mine. He told me he had a friend he'd like me to meet.

At that stage in my life, I was very down on men. I'd been stood up two weeks in a row and I thought all men were jerks and I didn't really want to meet anybody, particularly a jock. But Woody said something that intrigued me, something about how Bill was somehow different, more serious than most young men his age. I finally told Woody that if his friend really
(Continued)

wanted to meet me, that I'd be at the Black Night, a campus hangout, the following night after the basketball game.

Next night I walked into the place and saw Bill sitting at the end of the bar. I remember that I walked up behind him and said, "Hey Mac, you want to get married?" I remember Bill's comeback: "How about we dance first?"

We dated for a year, then got married while we were both still in college. By that time I'd transferred over to the University of Missouri. After college, we stayed on at Columbia while Bill served as a graduate assistant, then he got a job in St. Charles, and then it was on to Joplin.

One day Bill was on the telephone with his brother Tom, who told him about a job he thought Bill could get back in the Detroit area. So next morning, off we went in the car. We had one baby and I was very pregnant with our second child.

The early years were very confusing, very frustrating. We had a growing family and the life we were leading wasn't fitting into what my idea of marriage and family was all about. I had this Cinderella picture of what married life was supposed to be all about, yet here was my husband consumed with coaching and sports—and when he wasn't coaching, he was hanging around with guys talking about coaching. All I could think about was that if he really loved me, he wouldn't want to be with the guys.

At one point—I don't remember exactly when it was—I actually thought about leaving him. But then I thought how stupid it was. After all, I really loved him and besides, by that time we had three children, and where was I going to go

(Continued)

with three kids? I was so desperate—I kept trying to get his attention, and nothing was working. He was oblivious to it all.

Then I devised a scheme I thought would certainly get his attention.

I decided to drink.

One night I was watching Johnny Carson and I determined to get roaring drunk. So I got a shot of whisky and downed it in one gulp. Then I waited. Nothing happened. So I poured myself another shot and drank it. Still nothing happened. Then a third shot—yuk! It tasted terrible—and then a fourth. I was going to get drunk and let him find me that way and surely then I'd get his attention and he'd be concerned about me. Then he'd stay home more.

Suddenly it hit me. I was smashed.

My plan had been to drape myself on the stairway, where he'd have to step on me to get upstairs. I managed to get myself into position, lying with my feet pointing upstairs, so he might think I'd fallen down the stairs. Problem was, I couldn't wait him out. I got sicker and sicker lying upside down until I had to abandon the stairs for the bathroom. Then I went to bed. I had to put one foot outside the bed and onto the floor to try to keep the room from spinning. Nothing worked. I was paralyzed. Finally I passed out. Bill came home, undressed and crawled into bed, unaware of the dramatic stunt I had tried to pull off.

Not long ago, I told Bill that I wanted to try and give our

(Continued)

children a better start than we had. We were both so dumb, so unprepared for the realities of marriage and family. My concept was that my husband was going to be my partner, and it was a real shock to me that his career could possibly take up so much time—and that he would enjoy it so much to boot! Let's face it: he wasn't just dying to get home to me.

I know now that we both wanted the same thing but we didn't know how to get it, so we pulled against each other all the time. I'd whine and complain and say, "You don't love me anymore." That was offensive to him, causing him to withdraw from me.

But the one thing I've learned in my Christian walk is that if you have a strong foundation of faith in Jesus Christ, you can live through a sea of troubles. Believe me, we have come through a fire. Now, both of us want to make certain we live the right kind of life for our children, and set a good, Christian example for them. And when they find the person they want to share the rest of their life with, I'd like them to go away in a Christian environment and take a preparedness course for marriage. No books, no tapes. I want them to go through an entire marriage seminar. That way, they'd have a better chance of understanding the workings of a relationship—you know, all the kinds of things Bill and I didn't know in the first decade of our marriage.

the floor and looking up at all the big folks. During practice breaks, they'd be racing all around that gymnasium. Later on, they became ball boys for my team. Those were wondrous days, but unfortunately for most coaches and their children, there are far too few of them. With every coach I know, the major regret in their lives is that they did not spend enough time with their families. And in many cases, that absence has been very damaging.

Lyndi, thank God, has always been tolerant, always supportive. She's a godly woman who, in reality, has sacrificed her life for me. She has always been a giver, a woman who just wanted to make her man look good, to see me presented in a positive light even when I didn't deserve that kind of treatment.

I first met Lyndi when I was in college, and my first thought was that she was out of my league, perhaps too good for me. She was, and is, a very attractive woman. She just seemed to have it all. It's not that I thought I was a dumb jock—not at all. But I knew what I wanted to do with my life, and I knew it'd be a long struggle getting there. I simply thought she might be a little out of my reach. I was with my close friend Woody Widenhofer, then a football player at Missouri (now an assistant coach with the Detroit Lions) when we spotted Lyndi in a tea room in one of the buildings at Stephens College where she was going to school. Woody, who was also friends with Lyndi, pointed her out to me and he said, "See that girl over there? I'm gonna fix you up with her."

I told him to give it his best shot. "If you can get that done for me, I'll be indebted to you forever."

And I am.

But back then, even in the summer, instead of doing things with my family I would travel around the city and the suburbs with my players doing seven-on-seven passing drills, a practice that would later be outlawed by state officials. In the evenings, we would involve our basketball players with two leagues and various tournaments. The truth of it is, it was impossible for a kid who played sports for me to think about anything else but sports during the summer.

I had them five days a week.

The rationale behind it was simple: They wanted to be champions and wanted to earn scholarships to college—and many of them did. And I wanted to be a champion coach. We're talking here about a guy who was driven, who was obsessed, who was possessed. Did I take advantage of these young people? I hope I didn't. I like to feel that I got the most out of them. I extracted whatever they had to offer.

We lost only five games in four years of football. I'm not suggesting at all that I had earned a chance to coach at the collegiate level, but my eyes and my heart were pointed that way. And we had two all-state players that year and they certainly didn't damage my chances. Lots of major schools—including Michigan, Michigan State and Notre Dame—were recruiting our quarterback, Gary Forystek, and his favorite wide receiver, Ed Kasparek. You can imagine how many college recruiters were in and out of my office that season.

As it turned out, I got job offers not only from Michigan and Michigan State, but from Eastern Michigan University as well.

I was smart enough to know I was being courted not so much for my coaching skills as for the hope that where I went, my two star players would follow.

Denny Stolz was coaching at Michigan State back then and he wanted both our players. In one of his visits to our school he said, "I'm gonna tell you what I'm gonna do, Bill. I'm gonna find a job for you on my staff and I'm gonna hire you in September."

Then he flipped me forty dollars and said, "Take your wife to dinner."

This was in February, when the recruiting season gets to fever pitch. In the meantime, George Mans had gotten the head coaching job at Eastern Michigan, creating an opening on the Michigan staff. George called me and told me he'd like me to join the staff he was assembling at Eastern Michigan.

Schembechler had pretty much loaded up his staff with his pals from Ohio and endured some mild criticism for ignoring coaches in Michigan. It may be that Mans told Bo he was thinking about hiring me, because the next call I got was from Bo himself.

Even when he's trying to be gentle, Bo speaks in what some might term gruff tones.

"Coach, I have to fly to New York," he barked. "Make sure you don't take any job until I get back and get a chance to talk to you."

"Bo, you and I had better talk."

"Why?" he demanded.

"Well, Michigan State has offered me a job."

There was somewhat of a pause before he spoke again. "Where are you right now?" he wanted to know.

I told him I was in my office, right where he had called me.

"I'll be right there," he said and hung up.

Within the hour he barged into my office at the high school. He had known, he said, that Mans might offer me a job. As for Michigan State—his hated rival—all he could say was, "That's incredible."

> **Bo Schembechler wielded tremendous influence over his assistant coaches, and not because he tried to. He's just that powerful a personality, so imposing a force. Anyone with an ounce of sense would jump at the chance to work for him.**
> *Bill McCartney*

He paced back and forth for awhile, then said:

"I'll tell you what. I want you at Michigan. How much money are you making now?"

I was making about $16,000 but I had a few things on the side, so I stretched it out and told him I was making $19,000.

"I'll match that," said Schembechler.

I took the deal right on the spot.

Next duty was to tell Denny Stolz that I wouldn't be coming to Michigan State. I got him on the telephone but before I could blurt out the news of my decision, he told me he was coming to Divine Child to see my two athletes. When he arrived, he had two of his assistant coaches with him. I'm not sure he and the other coaches, Andy McDonald and Ed Youngs, even sat down before I just came right out with it:

"Denny, Bo offered me a job and I took it."

Stolz just looked at me. McDonald promptly got up and stalked out of the office and slammed the door.

"Hey," I tried to explain, "they've given me a full time job and I'm to report for work right away and I simply can't turn it down."

They just turned around and left my office. They weren't very happy, but they didn't say anything.

And I didn't give him back the forty bucks, either!

The two star players?

They both went to Notre Dame, recruited by Dan Devine, the man who had recruited me almost a generation before to play at University of Missouri.

When I learned that, I felt terrible about breaking the news to Schembechler, but Bo put his hand on my shoulder and offered some nice and consoling words:

"Let me just tell you this: a coach is worth ten players. Don't worry about it."

Maybe Bo was saying that to make me feel better, but it was nice, and at that time, I really needed to hear it.

The players never achieved stardom in big time football. Forystek beat out Joe Montana for the starting quarterback's job at Notre Dame, but suffered a fractured neck bone in a game against Purdue. Montana took over and never looked back. Kasparek ended up transferring to Michigan and playing some.

But I would hope they're better people today, and learned some valuable lessons about loyalty and teamwork and desire and dedication and determination—you know, all those things football coaches dwell on when they get into their cliché mode—from being in our football program.

I can assure you of this: I'm better off because they played so hard for me.

Seven

The Day that Changed My Life Forever

Bo Schembechler.

When I say that name today, it conjures up a lot of things. Like strength, leadership, grit, honesty—and yes, even humor. People who really don't know Glenn E. Schembechler rarely think of him as a humorous man, and it's true he didn't crack too many jokes early on in our relationship. It's just as true that if he could bully you and run over you and make you cringe, he'd do that, too. And he used those tactics on everyone, including members of the media.

I'm sure I've never met a more sincere man with as much clout and resolve as Bo had.

There's a Bible verse that fits Bo Schembechler to a tee: "He who rebukes a man will find more favor afterward than he who flatters with the tongue." (Prov. 28:23.) Bo's philosophy, on the field and off, was basic and simple: Confront everything, ignore nothing. He addressed every problem. Now. In the process, of course, he'd listen to his staff—but about half the time he wouldn't do what the rest of us suggested, because he'd already made up his mind what he was going to do.

A long time ago I read that there are different principles of leadership, and that one of them is that knowledge always translates into authority. You can bet that Bo was always informed. He wanted all the facts and he didn't want them colored nor softened. When he had the facts, he exercised tremendous authority. I know I've never met a tougher man, but because he blended fairness with toughness, he was forever able to rally those around him.

The other thing he always stressed was *team*. Never the individual, but the team. He preached it night and day and I'm sure he got a lot of that from when he coached under Woody Hayes at Ohio State. I'm persuaded that one of the reasons Michigan football teams were so successful over the years was that Schembechler didn't have superstars. There just wasn't room for them. The team was critical, the individual wasn't important. It was just like in a healthy family situation—no special privileges at home; everybody has a role; everybody has responsibilities; and they're all tied in to the general good of the family unit.

But despite this almost fanatical team doctrine, Bo inevitably was sensitive to individual needs. It seemed he had an eerie sort of sixth sense that enabled him to sniff out an individual problem. It can be an awful disruption to a team when players moan and complain all the time. Of course, there'll always be some of that when young men—who for the most part have been stars in high school—are competing for positions. Invariably, in the throes of a long and difficult season, individual problems will surface and grievances will be aired. Schembechler would confront, confront, confront. Those who were going to continue to be a problem were suppressed, and the blue chippers came through. Bo was firm, but I can say that he always tried to be fair.

Another great leadership quality was simply this: Bo knew how to make decisions; he never vacillated. Indecision creates confusion. It creates disharmony. And that wastes energy. Bo would size things up, then make a decision. You know, even a wrong decision can work for good if everybody is on the same page.

Finally, I always took note that Bo never varied in his recruiting strategy. It was always the same Bo—tough, hard, fair.

Oh, he knew some kids were being illegally recruited and that they and their parents were being offered inducements. And he knew that a favorite tack used by lesser teams was to tell a young man that he'd get lost in the shuffle at Michigan or Ohio State, because they had already corralled so many good players. Believe me, the truly outstanding players know in their hearts they're not going to get lost in anyone's shuffle. If I've heard Bo say it once I've heard it hundreds of times: "Let me tell you something, young man. I don't care what you've heard and I don't care what you've been promised somewhere else.

Bo Schembechler:

We had talked about Bill in staff meetings. He had a great reputation at Divine Child—and we had an opening at that time. As a rule, Michigan doesn't hire high school coaches. Usually the channel takes a coach from high school to a small college and then to a staff like Michigan's.

But Bill had spent a lot of time around our staff, we all knew him well, and I just thought he was that exceptional that he could make the jump from high school to a program like ours.

Turns out my judgment was pretty good, huh?

Here's what I'm telling you. I'm not giving you anything, but if you really have the right stuff, it'll surface at Michigan."

Gary Moeller, who recently succeeded Bo as head coach at Michigan, was the defensive coordinator when I joined the Michigan staff. He was patient with me and taught me a lot about football. My job was to coach the outside linebackers and we had a great staff and some great times. And we won a tremendous number of football games. Working on the staff of a powerful coach, in a successful program, often leads to great job opportunities.

It wasn't long before there occurred a job opening that intrigued me. Frank (Muddy) Waters was fired as head coach at Michigan State and there was some talk that I might be in line for the job. I confess that I openly campaigned for the job through the newspapers. Trust me when I tell you that didn't sit well with Bo.

"What kind of Michigan man are you?" he demanded to know. "What kind of a Michigan man would openly solicit a job at Michigan State?"

> **I had no reservations at all about giving Bill the job as defensive coordinator. He is good, he's hard working, he'll do whatever is necessary to get the job done. . .he's just good, that's all. I simply felt he was the best man for the job and I had no reservations about promoting him. That wasn't a tough decision.**
> *Bo Schembechler*

He was offended at what he considered a display of disloyalty to him and to the University of Michigan, and he was highly insulted that I would remotely entertain the thought of coaching the hated rivals from East Lansing. There still are a few Michigan people who think of Michigan State as a cow college.

I didn't make a fight out of it. I knew I had it coming. I was taken down a notch; I felt guilty about the whole thing and I apologized to him.

Don Canham was for many years the athletic director at the University of Michigan. It was Canham who hired Bo Schembechler and who is credited with being the creative genius who merchandised the Michigan athletic program into such an overwhelming popular and financial success that it has become the standard by which all other programs are gauged. Said Canham:

An athletic director, ninety-nine percent of the time, merely rubber stamps his coaches' staff selections. Sure, I'd heard of Bill McCartney because of his outstanding high school record in the Detroit area.

It didn't take long to get to know him. He's just one hell of a man, that's all. I liked him from the very start. Matter of fact, I'd have to say he was my favorite.

On road trips, I'd always try to sit beside him on the team plane because I enjoyed just talking with him. He's an absolute straight-shooter, with no sham or pretense about him. Sure, he was a great recruiter, and I'm sure it's because he has an aura of integrity about him the kids can spot.

He knows his stuff when it comes to coaching, and he exudes confidence. But the integrity, the candor, the honesty—those are the qualities that stick out. Those things make him a winner.

I don't miss much about being in charge of a mega-million dollar athletic facility. But I do miss the Bill McCartneys. I guess that's because you meet so few like that.

Three years after I got to Ann Arbor, Moeller was named head coach at Illinois and wanted me to accompany him as his defensive coordinator. I've always felt that when he went to Bo to ask permission to speak with me about it, that very conversation might have planted a seed in Bo's mind, because Bo didn't waste much time in naming me defensive coordinator at Michigan, in Moeller's place. It was a plum assignment and he selected me over some assistants who had been there longer and perhaps were more deserving.

He certainly didn't mince words when he approached me about my new assignment.

"You know you're gonna have to work a lot harder. You know I'll expect a lot more from you, don't you? Are you sure you're ready for this?"

I thought I was ready, and I prayed that I was right. Working hard had never been a problem for me. The only problem was the sometimes 100-hour-work week that I inflicted on my family.

And so I got a promotion, more responsibility, a greater challenge, more money. God was showering down all these blessings on me, and all the time I really didn't know it!

From the time I can first remember, I had what I thought was a good church life. From St. Cyprian's in the days of my childhood, to Divine Child in the early days of my coaching career, and then at St. Francis in Ann Arbor, I was a regular communicant and I was a believer. But there was something missing in my life and I had no clue what it was.

During my first season of coaching at Michigan, I was curiously drawn to a particular player. There was something about him that set him apart. He was a player of outstanding abilities with a great work ethic. He was a tough kid with a ready smile and a serenity and peace about him that belied his youth.

Chuck Heater was solidly built with 205 pounds on his six-foot frame. It was said at the time that he was the fastest fullback

Michigan ever had. Chuck had been a prep all-American at Tiffin Columbia High School in Ohio and made the all-Big Ten second team as a junior. I approached Heater one day in practice and said, "You really seem to have it all together—just what is it about you?"

This poised young man acted almost as if he had been expecting such a question.

"Tell you what, Coach. We're going to have a conference in a few days up at Brighton and I'd like you to come."

I agreed. The night before the conference, I was up 'til two in the morning, but I slept fast. I felt pretty good the next morning, but was still glad I had talked Coach Moeller into driving up with me.

In the room that Sunday morning were eighteen Michigan athletes from various sports. Lots of them were our football players. The guy running the meeting was Dennis Painter, then the area director for Athletes in Action, a branch of Campus Crusade for Christ.

That day, for the first time in my life, I was confronted with questions about my faith. Did I have a personal relationship with Jesus Christ? Had I surrendered control of my life to Jesus? Had I made him Lord of my life?

As Dennis stood at the podium and talked, it dawned on me that my answer to all of the questions he was posing was "No." Sure, I believed in Jesus Christ—but I had no idea how His Word could work in my life. I hadn't turned the reins of my life over to Him. I knew He had richly blessed me, but I hadn't done very much for Him at all.

I began to realize something else, too. When the people in that room got up and talked about Scripture, they spoke intimately of things that were foreign to me. I had never been encouraged to read the Bible, so I knew nothing about the Word of God and what it could mean to me. I had no idea what great new direction it could give to me and my family!

That morning, as several young athletes gave their testimonies, everything began to come into focus for me. They talked about the fact that the Bible was written by thirty-six authors over fifteen hundred years—yet it was as if these thirty-six authors sat down at the same table and wove it together, because every word— inspired by God—fits together perfectly. One young man said there were more than eight-hundred promises in that book—it was all news to me!

In summary, I began to realize that I had been totally without a clue about what it's like to be a whole-hearted, committed Christian—to have the true spirit of the Lord in my heart.

Right then and there, I made a decision. I decided to commit my life to Jesus Christ.

You see, I've always been a whole-hearted guy, and I've always wanted a full-measure of whatever was out there. I've never wanted just part of the package, part of the prize. I want it all! Over the previous ten years I'd been a daily communicant in the Catholic Church. You don't have that kind of resolve unless you want something really enthusiastically. I knew I wanted a deeper walk with the Lord. And that day, I realized what I had been missing—I hadn't been born again!

I wanted more. I wanted all of it. Right then and there, I prayed hard to receive the full measure of God's love. It was the most exciting moment of my life!

Dennis Painter agreed to meet with me alone later that morning. We also agreed to meet again soon and schedule some follow-up visits. Suddenly, I was on fire, and thirsty for the knowledge of the Lord.

I hardly remember the drive home. I do remember that when I got there, Lyndi was talking with a lady friend of hers in our living room. I burst in the front door, unable to wait to tell her the news.

"This morning I did something really exciting!" I interrupted. Lyndi looked up, an expectant look on her face. I continued: "I committed my life to Jesus Christ!"

Lyndi's smile went limp. I went on to tell how I'd realized I never had a full and personal relationship with Jesus Christ—but that now I was on the right track!

The two women just sat there, staring at me, not comprehending the full meaning of what I was trying to share. I waited for a response; there was none. Finally, I just excused myself and left the room.

The other woman jabbed Lyndi in the ribs. "Don't worry about it," she said. "I've seen this sort of thing before. It blows right over."

That was 1974 and nothing has blown over except a lot of troubles, because every day since that warm summer morning in Brighton, Michigan, my love for the Lord has grown along with my desire to serve him.

There was no dramatic, bolt-of-lightening turnaround in my life. Everything good that has happened has come about gradually, as I have grown spiritually. Morning after morning, Dennis Painter and I would meet at sunup in a fast food restaurant in Ann Arbor. He saw my enthusiasm, my desire to put on the whole armor of God, and he fed me spiritually.

One day he gave me a Bible, and when I looked at it, I noticed it did not have the Latin words *Nihil Obstat* printed on the cover. So I knew it hadn't been authorized by the Catholic Church.

I shook my head and handed the book back to Dennis. "I can't read it," I told him.

"It doesn't matter if those words are there," Dennis responded. "This is the Bible!"

"Well, I'm just telling you I can't read it."

The next morning, he came back with two Bibles. They were identical, except that one had the Latin words on its front. So I began the great, exciting adventure of reading God's Word, aided by a basic study guide Dennis had given me on how to read the Bible and understand it better.

Not long afterwards, I ran into Bishop Joseph McKinney of Grand Rapids, Michigan and, my voice edged with excitement, I said, "Bishop McKinney, I have an important question for you, and how you answer could affect me for the rest of my life."

Nodding, he told me to pop the question.

"I believe I'm a born-again Catholic," I blurted. "What's your reaction to that?"

"I think you are, too."

I pursued the issue. "Yes, but—well, what do you think about it?"

"That's okay. That's absolutely okay."

Then I told him I had made a personal decision to invite Jesus into my life, to make Him Lord of my life.

And he just said, "Great. That's great."

Making a profession of faith like I did may not be expected and may not even be important in the Catholic Church, but it's important to me, because it says to do so in the Bible.

Lyndi was not a Catholic when we married. I insisted that we be married in the Catholic Church but we didn't have a mass. We had married as we were finishing up our college work at Missouri, and when I took my first teaching/coaching job in St. Charles, a suburb of St. Louis, Lyndi converted to Catholicism. More than anything else, I believe it was born out of a desire on her part that we worship together.

Well, within a year after I made my commitment to follow Jesus Christ, Lyndi made her own decision to follow Him. She'll be the first to tell you that it wasn't a bells-and-whistles conversion: it was done quietly, in her own timing. Our kids were between the ages of three and eleven at the time, and I have no question that when Lyndi and I became partners in our faith in Jesus Christ, it established a new dimension in our home—a new depth that, thirteen years later, would be the very foundation enabling us to endure the hardships that we faced.

Lyndi McCartney:

When Bill and I got married, I became a Catholic just to please him. I was so madly in love with him I'd have jumped through burning hoops to please him, but I also believed the family should worship together, in one place. As my children grew older and went to Catholic school, I naturally became more involved in church goings-on, particularly once we got to Ann Arbor. But my life was more school-centered than church-oriented. I guess it's safe to say I never found a "home" in the Catholic Church.

The day Bill came home from that meeting in Brighton and announced to my girl friend and me that he had been born again, my friend was able to shrug it off but I didn't know what to make of it.

Bill is a one hundred percent guy. Whatever he does, he does with great zeal. He goes all the way, sometimes to the exclusion of everything else. I basically had no idea what he was talking about.

As time went on, I thought he was downright obnoxious about it. Every time he turned around, he was praising the Lord for everything. I remember one bitter cold December day when I had to do some Christmas shopping, so I got all bundled up and took the baby with me, and went to this discount warehouse. Once inside, you had to go all through this maze before you could escape, and it was bedlam. I was hot and tired and the baby was cranky and they didn't have anything I wanted and by the time I got home I was very frustrated. Well, the minute I hit the door, Bill sang out,

(Continued)

'Well, praise the Lord.' I just freaked! I told him he could praise the Lord for anything he wanted, but by all means, don't praise Him for my troubles! I was furious!

Instead of not knowing where I was in my faith at that time, I knew—I simply wasn't anywhere. But Alice Painter, then wife of Dennis Painter who had helped lead Bill to the Lord, kept dogging me about making a fresh start in Christ. She really was relentless and sometimes it bugged me that she was so determined.

One afternoon we were at my house and she asked, "Do you know if you're going to Heaven?" I told her yes, but that I didn't want to talk about it any more.

The truth was, I didn't know the answer. I had no real basis for having that blessed assurance. As a child, I had gone to a Methodist Church, but I don't recall any real emphasis on Scripture. I had nothing inside me that could prove I was a child of God. I assumed that nice people go to Heaven, I thought I was nice enough, so I figured that just about did it. I was into being a nice person; Jesus was not a living savior to me.

For months I had been resenting Alice because she kept pounding away and making me think. But when she left that afternoon—and I remember it was about five o clock and I was in the house all by myself—I sat down on my bed and invited the Lord into my life.

There was no bolt of lightning, no clap of thunder, no giant sign of peace. I kept thinking, "All right, Lord, I've done it. Now what?" I can't say what I expected, but I sat there for a

(Continued)

while. Then I just said, "Lord, I can't wait forever. I have to finish getting dinner."

I'm sure I was a changed person from that day forward, because I knew beyond the shadow of a doubt that I had made a significant change in my thinking, and I didn't have to experience some miraculous, overt demonstration to prove it. I came to understand that God works in different ways with different people. One of the first things I wanted to do was to study the Word

Several months earlier, Alice Painter had given me a workbook she had written, entitled *The Challenge of Being a Woman: God's Way to Freedom and Fulfillment.* I'd never bothered to look at it, but now suddenly I began to read, and then to understand, about the meaning of God's Word and His will. Soon I began to develop as a Christian and to have more peace within myself. There was a great calming that took place, and that was the beginning for Bill and me to have a deeper, better relationship within our marriage.

This may sound terrible, but I didn't tell Bill about my decision right away. Maybe I thought Bill would make a big deal out of it, but for me, it was a matter of seed-planting, and I needed to grow. It really was a simple matter of faith.

Later, we went to several Fellowship of Christian Athlete's summer camps, and those were periods of real spiritual growth that, for one thing, made our marriage a lot healthier. Still, it took many years to realize that Bill and I are just different; God called us to different gifts. Still, we pray to the same Person, and I have confidence that God knows what is best for us, because we are His children.

(Continued)

It's a good thing I have read and re-read about all the tribulations, the afflictions—almost curses, it seems—that have rained down on some of the truly remarkable Christians in Biblical days. I've had my doubts and fears, my periods of despair when I've thrown up my hands. And I've sometimes looked to Heaven and asked, "God, are you sure you have the right address here? Are you positive we have to go through this?"

But God always brings us through. Of course, it isn't a radical, overnight occurrence—it's a gradual but definite transformation. After all, a diamond doesn't turn brilliant and well-cut with one buffing. Similarly speaking, it takes God's grace and a lot of hard work on our part to turn a life around.

Eight

My Personal Cross

*What does not destroy me,
strengthens me.*
—*Nietzsche*

I never thought for one minute that when I changed the course of my spiritual life, my troubles were behind me. Although I admit that in weaker moments, I sometimes cry out in my own personal anguish and get into my "Why me, God?" mode. Like everyone else, I think I am sometimes singled out for heavy crosses.

In my infancy with Jesus Christ, I became involved in a Bible study group. There were seven couples at our home for the first meeting. There was big-time tension in the room. Just to get things started, Lyndi and I asked the others, "Well, why are you here?"

Virtually everyone responded the same way. They all said things like, "I'm just here to check this thing out," or "I'm not saying we're coming back," or "We're here because you invited us."

Dennis Painter had given me a Bible study tape, a study

booklet and a Bible. To get started, we listened to the tape for about two minutes, until the voice said, "Okay, shut me off now, and open up to page one in the booklet." And we were off and running. It was the most basic, elementary stuff—like a kindergarten course—but it struck home with all of us. It was a diverse group: friends, neighbors, people I'd grown up with. Some were Catholic and some were Protestant. We met every other Saturday for one year, and to mark our first anniversary we got together for dinner and study in a friend's home in Southgate, Michigan.

After dinner, the men went downstairs to talk, and I said, "Do you guys realize how much our lives have changed in the past year? Not a one of us is the same. I'll tell you point-blank—I don't see enough of you guys."

We agreed then and there to find a place where we could gather—just the guys—every week for breakfast and prayer and fellowship. Early on we met at Sambo's restaurant in Taylor, a forty-five minute drive from my house. I got up on those mornings at 4:45 a.m. to get to our breakfasts by 6:15, then made a mad dash back to Ann Arbor because our football meetings began at 8:00 a.m. Seven men attended our first breakfast. Then the word began to spread. Someone would invite somebody else and soon there were twenty men. Then forty. We shared openly about our fears and the struggles in our lives, inviting outside speakers to share with us as our numbers began to grow. Sixty, eighty, a hundred—before long the little room in that restaurant was bursting at the seams.

They came from every walk of life. There were businessmen alongside construction workers, truck drivers alongside white collar executives. And I began to see what God can do with a surrendered heart. Sure, there were guys who checked us out just once or twice, then checked out themselves. Maybe they'd seen someone in there they considered a hypocrite. Many stayed, though, and participated, and grew spiritually. Before long I was bringing a car full of men with me from Ann Arbor. One day, one of them suggested that rather than drive the forty-five minutes to Taylor each Tuesday morning, we should begin another prayer breakfast right there in Ann Arbor. There were only a handful at the onset but like the Taylor meeting, the Ann Arbor session began to explode until we had sixty men in attendance every Thursday morning.

I was burning the candle at both ends, but I was getting so much reinforcement that I was on fire for the Lord. And God's spirit was moving through this entire group, both in Taylor and in Ann Arbor.

But Bill McCartney was living a lie! My lifestyle wasn't in keeping with the commitment I'd made. I was a drinker!

Not a mad, raving, falling down drunk, mind you—and not an abusive, bellowing drunk—but a man who constantly had to battle a desire to drink. I'd go seven, eight days or longer, without having so much as a beer, and then I'd drink. Afterward, I'd be consumed by guilt.

Now I'm not sitting in judgement, condemning those who take an occasional drink—I realize they didn't have Welch's grape juice at the Last Supper—but Lyndi and I both had endured enough incidents, seen enough signals to know that we'd both be better off if I just ordered a diet cola. I was never physically abusive to her nor to the children—but our biggest disputes, our great times of contention, came about when I was drinking. Some guys get melancholy when they drink; some guys get romantic. But I just got belligerent.

After the 1975 season, our Michigan team was invited to play Oklahoma in the Orange Bowl at Miami, and Oklahoma won the game and the national championship. One of the events I attended there in Florida was a breakfast meeting hosted by the Fellowship of Christian Athletes. The main speaker was Steve Davis, the twenty-one-year-old quarterback for Oklahoma, and an ordained Baptist preacher. He told some cute stories and the young people laughed, and he was making a nice presentation when suddenly he sort of shouted into the microphone:

"When are you going to take a stand? When are you going to stand up and be counted for Jesus Christ?"

Those words, it seemed, were aimed straight at me. Yes, I had made a commitment and yes, I was growing as a Christian and yes, I was living a contradiction. That morning, I rededicated myself to gaining the strength to overcome the temptation to drink.

From Miami, I went to the American Football Coaches' Association convention in St. Louis. Grant Teaff had done a great job at Baylor and he'd been named coach of the year and would be honored at the meeting. I had run into some of my old Missouri buddies, and one of them wanted to go to the coach of the year dinner with me. I knew he'd had quite a bit to drink, and looking back, I know I shouldn't have taken him. We hadn't even been served, and my buddy was staring holes through Coach Teaff. For reasons I can't ascertain to this day, he was ready to fight Teaff, and he didn't even know him. I got him out of there, sent him home and that night I went to my room and knelt by my bedside to pray for deliverance from my temptation to drink. Up to that time, I had equated having a few drinks with having a good time. But I was finally I beginning to face the fact that I cannot drink in moderation. Whenever there had been a cocktail party—and there are lots of them everywhere—I'd always had a drink, then two, then three. I've never been one to merely nurse a drink. If I could be temperate, I wouldn't have a problem.

The words Steve Davis spoke were still ringing in my ears as I got down to pray. Here I knew that I was telling people that I was a Christian, but my life was not supporting that. For three years after that night, I did not touch a single drop of alcoholic beverage. But oh, how I was put to the test.

A few months later, Jerry Hanlon, who'd been coaching with Bo for many years, and I went to Arkansas to study the Razorbacks' program. Jimmy Johnson (later coach of the Miami Hurricanes and now coach of the Dallas Cowboys of the NFL) was the defensive coordinator at that time and he showed us around.

Jimmy's a gregarious, fun-loving, personable guy. I couldn't be more impressed with his knowledge of football. And he seemed genuinely excited to have two coaches from Bo Schembechler's staff to show around. A little later, we went into a bar and everyone ordered beers all around, and when the waitress asked for my order, I didn't know if I would be able to say *no*. I really wanted a cold one, but finally I said, "I'll take a Coke."

And that was it. Doing that, that day, somehow freed me of a lot of my temptation. I had been worried about the pressure from others. I had been too concerned about what others would think of me, instead of what the Lord thinks of me. God surely knows booze is a problem for me, and for me to sit there and drink Coke while they pounded down a couple of beers—it may not seem like a significant step to those who can take it or leave it

Jon Falk joined the University of Michigan football program as the equipment manager in 1974, the same year Bill McCartney arrived:

Even though I had known Bo Schembechler from my days at Miami University in Oxford, Ohio, it was a bit overwhelming coming to Michigan. I had worked with some of the other assistant coaches when Bo was at Miami, but McCartney was brand new.

Right away, you could tell he was different. And I was drawn to him. He was very open and friendly, but very serious. A very decent guy, he had a genuine commitment to the football players. He was devoted to them, and cared about them as people. He communicated well with them and was a unifying factor, especially among the younger players who were away from home for the first time, who were intimidated and sometimes frightened.

(Continued)

alone. But if you or someone you love has ever understood that it can be a major problem, you will know something of what I experienced that day.

A long time ago, a friend of mind told a banquet story about the Irishman who passed the local pub on his way home from work each evening. Problem was, he could never really "pass" it. He stopped daily, and stayed until he could hardly find his way home. When he finally got there, he'd berate his wife and kids, sober up and apologize the next morning, and then go do it all over again. Finally during one sobering session in the confessional, he blurted out his guilt to the local priest.

"You must be strong, my son," the priest advised him. "You must not stop at the pub. You have to walk right up to that place, stiffen your shoulders and stride right by. You must be of firm resolve and you must be convicted in your heart this is the proper thing to do."

The very next evening, our Irishman left work and headed home, and when he got beside the pub, he straightened himself and muttered, "Patty, today we're going to go right past that evil place." And lo and behold, he did. And when he took about four or five paces and got in front of the butcher shop, he paused, then said:

"Ah, well done, Patty me boy. That wasn't so hard now, was it? Come on back lad, and I'll treat you to a pint."

For the most part, I've been able to pass the pub, and to keep right on walking. Ever since that night in St. Louis, I have mainly had victory over alcohol. Don't read into this that I haven't been tempted, because I have, and mightily. The Lord has said He will withhold no good thing, but I believe the Lord's message to me is that I drank too much when I was a young man, that drinking is cumulative, and that drinking is a problem for me. So I constantly pray for the courage to keep right on walking.

I don't sit in judgment of a Christian who takes a drink. I merely have to recognize the unalterable fact that Bill McCartney has a drinking problem and it's one that I fight all the time. In the past, I have viewed drinking as a form of relaxation, something that takes the edge off when the pressure is on. But every time I have relented and had a drink, I have tremendous turmoil down deep in my soul. The Lord has convicted me that I really do have a drinking problem—it ain't gonna go away. The Lord has said to me, "I'm not going to absolve you of that. This is your cross. You are going to be around cocktail parties and people who drink all of you life, and you simply have to abstain."

I go through times when I break down and I do have a drink, and then I go through pure hell. I'm whole hearted. I want to be right with the Lord. I must be clean before Him.

Someone once suggested that I might be suffering from a "religious hangover" because of my Catholic upbringing and because of the fact that in my thirties I was born again and came to

I was single at the time, and I didn't have anyone to go to church with, and Bill reached out to me. When I'd swear, he'd very quietly remind me that I didn't have to use those words— and he always did it with a nice smile.

We jogged together, and I was always out of shape, and I'd be gasping for breath and ready to give up and find a soft spot to lie down. He'd just keep on jogging, and then turn to me and say, "You know, Jon, we're very fortunate. Think of the people who can't walk, who can't breathe. Think what they'd give just to be able to be out here like we are right now. We really have a lot to be thankful for, you know."

Then I'd change my mind about quitting. He has that affect on people, and he's most persuasive because he leads by precept and example, not just by talking about it.

know Jesus Christ as my personal Saviour.

Let me set a couple things straight. I'm not flailing away at myself to atone for some terrible sins committed way back when. I'm not concealing any horrendous sin and covering myself up with the cloak of religion to keep that dark secret hidden forever. I've heard about as many stories as I need to about Catholic guilt and I'm not sure it's any different than Jewish guilt or Baptist guilt. Sin is sin, and guilt is guilt, and when I fall short of the glory of God, I have a conscience and I feel bad about it.

But here's the good news. Even though I fall short, it's still possible to strive to live a life fully committed and glorifying to Jesus Christ. No matter what struggles dot my past, I can endure all things, living victorious for God.

Take Paul, for example. I've spent a lot of time reading Bible stories about this remarkable man. He began as the bitterest enemy the Gospel had. He was a murderer, a bigot, he hated Christianity and everything about it and he almost single-handedly drove the church out of Jerusalem. And he was on his way to Damascus to do the same thing there—to find Christians and bind them and bring them back to a kangaroo court and put them to death. Then, at the doorway of Damascus, the Lord Jesus Christ appeared to him in person and struck him down and transformed his life. From then on, Paul was a completely changed man. All his old war buddies, his cronies, were amazed. They couldn't understand what had happened to him. But he stayed true all the rest of his days.

In II Corinthians, there's a list as long as a tall man's arm relating all the things Paul endured. He was beaten, stoned, shipwrecked three times, imprisoned, and there were many attempts on his life before he was finally killed, beheaded in Rome because of his love for the Gospel. And just before the end of his life, he was able to write to Timothy: "I have fought the good fight, I have finished the race, I have kept the faith. Finally, there is laid up for me the crown of righteousness, which the Lord, the righteous Judge, will give to me on the Day, and not to me only but also to all who have loved His appearing." (II Tim. 4:7-8.)

Paul said in Colossians that Christ is our life and in Galatians that Christ lives in us and again in Colossians that Christ in us is the hope of glory. I want more than anything in the world for Jesus Christ to live out His life through me. Without Him I am nothing; with Him I have the promise of everlasting life. Is there any better deal you can cut? Does anything else give you that assurance? It boggles my mind that someone can see life breathed into a baby, watch the grass die and then come to life again, see leaves fall and watch the rebirth of a tree, or gaze on any of the majestic splendor that is this earth and not be overpowered by the presence of an Almighty God!

One of my dearest friends in all the world—when I told him I was going to do this book and withhold nothing—cautioned me about the dangers of total candor. No need to bring up that abortion controversy again, he argued. Why dig up this matter of Kristy and Sal and the baby once more? What's the point in resurrecting the problems some of your players have had in the past with the police?

Here's the point, and it's the only thing that really matters:

"For our boasting is this: the testimony of our conscience that we conducted ourselves in the world in simplicity and godly sincerity, not with fleshly wisdom but by the grace of God, and more abundantly toward you."

That's II Corinthians, first chapter, verse twelve.

It works for me.

Bill McCartney and his wife, Lyndi, at the 1989 season celebration.

McCartney with sons Mike and Tom, in their days of playing basketball at Gabriel Richard High School.

McCartney and his family arrived in Colorado to coach the Buffaloes in 1982. (Clockwise from upper left) Mike, Bill, Tom, Marc, Kristy, and Lyndi.

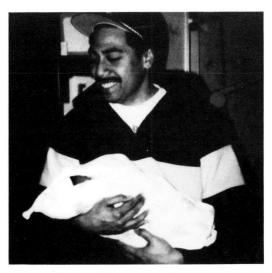

The late Sal Aunese holds newborn Timothy Chase.

William Patrick McCartney and Ruth Lloyd McCartney, Bill's parents and biggest fans. They taught him to value integrity and discipline.

Bill McCartney, a baby in Riverview, Michigan.

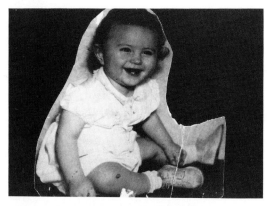

The house on Reno Street, where Bill grew up.

High school graduation.

Bill was captain of the football team at Riverview High School.

Center-Linebacker for the University of Missouri, 1959–1961, Bill graduated with a degree in education in 1962.

McCartney's 1970 basketball team.

Hired by head football coach Tony Versaci, McCartney's coaching career was boosted when he came to Dearborn Divine Child High School in 1969 as assistant football coach and head basketball coach.

The coach calls the play.

The 1973 basketball team went all the way to the Michigan State Class B championship and won.

Coach Bo Schembechler (left) spoke at the Divine Child High School awards banquet. Father Herm Kucyk sits at the right.

Bill was assistant football coach his four years at Divine Child.

Bill's first year on staff at the University of Michigan. Bill's gained invaluable experience in his years under Coach Schembechler.

Photography by Laura Larson

Photography by Dan Madden

Coach McCartney in action as the Buffalo coach. Colorado had won only 7 games in its last 3 seasons when McCartney came to be head football coach in 1982. He began a rebuilding program that took the team to its 1989 "Golden Season."

The Buffaloes salute
Sal Aunese before
the Missouri game.

Photography by Ed Kosmicki

*Four years into McCartney's
rebuilding program, the Buffaloes
broke a 20-year losing streak
against Nebraska. Here, in 1989,
the Buffalo teammates hoist Coach
McCartney on their shoulders
after a 27–21 win against the
Cornhuskers. This was the first
time in 66 years that Colorado
had a 9–0 season start.*

*The coach paces the sidelines during the 1989
Oklahoma game.*

McCartney shows confidence in press conferences before the 1990 Orange Bowl.

The Buffalo coach accepts his Kodak Coach of the Year plaque from 1989 AFCA president Don James of the University of Washington, at a press conference held during the AFCA convention.

Nine

His Rock in Boulder

Had I been in Eddie Crowder's shoes in June of 1982, I would not have hired me to coach football at Colorado University. But I'm not, and he did. For the longest time, it looked to most people like a classic boner. When Chuck Fairbanks resigned as Colorado Coach on June 1, 1982, he left behind a nose-diving program in turmoil, and academicians in a state of unrest about the large number of football players who were either not graduating, or flunking out. Fairbanks left to coach the New Jersey Generals of the fledgling United States Football League.

The timing could not have been worse. Anyone who currently had a head coaching job would have been embarrassed and probably damaged back home had he applied for the Colorado job and not gotten it. Plus, at that time of year, most college coaches are either taking family vacations or doing clinics. They're already thinking of the work that lies ahead the first of August when you begin serious preparations for the next campaign.

Like everyone else, I'd heard about Fairbanks' departure but I had no thought of applying for the job. The word was out almost immediately that Drake coach Chuck Shelton had the inside track on the job. After all, he had beaten Colorado twice in a row. Besides, I was afraid to go after the job. My major concern was how Bo Schembechler would take it. We were getting set to move into high gear for the 1982 season at Michigan, and the old man might growl more than a little if I threw my hat into the ring. It would look like I was abandoning ship, and at a critical time, to boot.

Tony Versaci, who'd given me my first big break by practically hand-picking me as his successor at Dearborn Divine Child High School, telephoned to ask if I'd thought about applying for the position. I told him all the negatives, how I was worried about Bo's reaction, and that I'd decided to stay where I was. Tony wanted to know if it would be all right for him to call Eddie Crowder at Colorado on my behalf.

Now, Tony Versaci is a dynamic and persuasive man, but I doubted that Eddie Crowder had ever heard of him, and it gave every appearance of a wasted effort. But I told him to call if he wanted to.

Crowder had coached Colorado to some of its greatest victories in eleven seasons, and now he had been athletic director for a good number of years. He would tell me later that he'd had a huge stack of messages on his desk when his eyes somehow fell on the one from Tony Versaci. I guess it was about the only name he didn't recognize. He called, and Tony gave me such a glowing buildup that Eddie felt compelled to at least check me out. Eddie called Schembechler to get permission to talk to me, and Bo told him I'd do a good job for him.

Crowder and I made phone connections at about eleven o clock one Sunday night, and he asked me when I could come to Boulder for a visit. I was on a flight at six the next morning. There were writers and photographers all over the place when I stepped off the plane, but throughout that whole day I got the feeling that Crowder wasn't overly impressed with me. I began to fear I was nothing more than a token interview.

I called Lyndi late that night and we prayed together. I specifically remember saying, "Lord, I know You wouldn't send me all the way to Boulder, Colorado for a token interview. I'm believing that's not the way things are going to happen, and I'm praying that You will give me favor with Eddie Crowder as well as with the other people here. Amen."

I enjoyed dinner with Eddie and his wife, Jean. The next morning, Eddie had set up a series of meetings. At ten I was scheduled to meet with a variety of people involved in the search: faculty, an alumni representative, someone from the community. As I recall, there were about a dozen people involved.

At quarter to ten, I was pacing around in an outer office, waiting for the meeting to begin. I noticed that Fred Casotti was doing some work at a nearby desk. Now, Fred had been the sports information director at Colorado for a long time, and later became one of Crowder's right hand men. He's a man with a wry sense of humor, and since he'd been around the CU program for thirty years, he could afford to say exactly what was on his mind.

For some reason, I turned and asked, "Fred, what do you think my chances are?"

He sort of peered at me over his glasses and said, "Coach, it's third and long. You'd better make a big play."

Maybe he felt bad that he'd been so blunt with me, so he added, "Hey, you're from Michigan. Take that in there with you. That's a great place."

The format of the meeting called for me to answer questions, but before anyone could ask me anything, I stood up and just plain talked for about fifteen minutes. I told them what I would bring to Colorado. I spoke about Michigan's great program for athletic accomplishment and academic integrity, and that Colorado could expect the same thing from me. As it turned out, they really didn't ask me any questions. I knew then I was at least in the ball game.

They had arranged for me to have lunch with a group of men from the community who wanted to check me out. One of them was Joe Romig, who had been not only an all-American on the field, but an academic all-American as well. I felt good about that session, too.

In the afternoon, I met with Dr. Arnold R. Weber, then the president of the university. He asked me some basic questions. The whole meeting was very low key, very cordial. He's a no-nonsense man, bright and resourceful, a sort of a Bo Schembechler of college presidents. Finally, I said to him:

"President Weber, there's something you should know. Football is not the most important thing in my life. It's not even second. It's a distant third. I've committed my life to Almighty God. My wife and children are my second priority, and football's third. If Colorado should offer me this job, you should know what you're getting."

It happened that the Board of Regents was meeting in Denver, and I went by just to meet them, not really to say anything. I was there only briefly and never even sat down, but one member of the board asked if there was anything I wanted to say.

> I knew McCartney was going to stand right up in the marketplace and say, "I am a Christian." Some people would recoil at that, but I understood that a man who lives by the creed of his faith is going to conduct the program properly in the best interests not only of the institution but of the athlete.
>
> *Eddie Crowder*

And I told them the exact same thing I had told Dr. Weber, that Jesus Christ was Lord of my life, that my family came second and that football was a distant third. When Fred Casotti and I walked out of there, he suggested we drive back to Boulder and grab a bite of dinner. When we got in the car, I asked Fred again how he assessed my chances.

"Coach, it's fourth and short. You're in this thing."

Tony Versaci, now a successful businessman, coached foot-ball at Dearborn Divine Child High School for eleven sea-sons, and in that span of years, the teams he coached lost only seven games. Said Versaci:

I told Bill he should go after the job but he was reluctant. He was worried about the timing, about leaving the Michigan program with the staff having everything in place for the 1982 season. I don't think he gave a thought to it being an equally bad time to go to Colorado since he'd miss out on a whole recruiting season there.

When I called for Eddie Crowder, I didn't get through to him, but left a message with his secretary. That was on a Wednesday. Normally I don't go to my office on Saturdays, but that week I decided to take my son in, just to show him where his daddy works. The phone rang, and it was Crowder.

I don't know how long we talked. No, make that how long I talked because when we finally hung up, I realized I had talked almost non-stop. About all Crowder got to say was "Yes" or "Okay" or "Uh huh." I wore him out, but I had a lot of good things to say about Bill and I didn't want to leave any of them out.

Crowder told me years later that after listening to me for ten minutes, he would have agreed to interview Bill just to get me off the phone, and after half an hour he was ready to give the job to me!

Later that night, Eddie Crowder called me in my hotel room and offered me the job. I told him I wanted it, but that I'd have to return to Michigan and discuss it with my family. I flew back on Wednesday, received a unanimous "yea" vote from Lyndi and the four kids, called Crowder and accepted the job. Lyndi and I flew back to Colorado on Thursday for the formal announcement.

Within days, I had two affirmations that the entire matter was orchestrated by God.

I had been enjoying a warm fellowship with the Word of God Community in Ann Arbor and went to a community gathering to say my goodbyes. There must have been twenty-five hundred people in an auditorium in nearby Ypsilanti that night, and as I was bidding them farewell, a man stood up in the congregation and said:

"Bill, I have a message to you from the Lord. The Lord is sending you to Boulder, Colorado, and you will be His rock in Boulder."

Soon after I returned to Boulder a second time, a woman in one of the Eastern states wrote me and said, "Almighty God told me to write you and tell you that He was sending you to Boulder, Colorado, and that you will be His rock in Boulder."

I have neither seen nor heard from those people since, but I took those messages as affirmation that this job came about by Divine Appointment. Not only that, I believe that everything that has happened since then—the wonderful things and the awful things, as well—occurred not by happenstance but through the will of God.

Three of our four children were eager to pull up stakes and move to Boulder. Mike was the starting quarterback at Gabriel Richard High School in Ann Arbor but he was ready for a larger challenge at a bigger school in Boulder. Kristyn and Marc were younger and at an age where every day is exciting and challenging, so they were ready for anything. But Tom dragged his feet. Even though he was a fullback and a linebacker and had been a starter, too, at Gabriel Richard baseball had always been Tom's first love. When I took the job in Boulder, Tom was playing on a great sandlot team in a well-structured league in Ann Arbor. He was a pretty good pitcher, played infield and was a good hitter. I hurt for his sense of loss at leaving; but I knew he'd have to find a way to adjust.

Even before we arrived in Boulder, there had been considerable fanfare about the arrival of the new athletes on the scene—the McCartney boys. There'd been a pretty good tradition established on that front. Doug Dickey, for example, had been on Chuck Fairbanks' staff and his son was good enough to become the starting quarterback at Tennessee; Bill Mallory had coached at Colorado and his sons were outstanding athletes who went on to play for Bo Schembechler at Michigan; Fairbanks' son Toby got a football scholarship at Michigan State. It would be an underestimate to say that a coaches' son would be expected to excel in Boulder.

Immediately when my family arrived in town, my older sons were put on the same American Legion baseball team. The first crisis came before Lyndi even had the house in order: Before the first week was up, the boys' team was playing a team from Denver and the kid pitching for Denver was a whiz. He was rangy, had a moustache and just kept blowing the ball past the Boulder kids. He was simply overpowering.

In the sixth inning of that game, Tom went to bat with the bases loaded and two outs. I was in the stands, fervently praying that he'd acquit himself well so he'd be accepted by his new teammates. Coming to Boulder had been hard on him. All I wanted was for Tom to have a little success because I knew how much he was hurting. I wanted him to feel that he had a place in Boulder as well as in Ann Arbor.

Doggoned if he didn't jerk one right over the fence for a grand slam home run!

It was a gift from God that went a long way toward helping Tom make new friends and begin to feel better about himself. It was the greatest tonic he could have had.

Bill McCartney:

Following Boulder High, our son Mike was recruited by Washburn College in Topeka and became the starting quarterback. But after two-and-a-half years, he wanted to come back home and finish his degree at Colorado. After graduation, he became one of my graduate assistants, and as this book goes to press, is being considered for positions at several major universities.

Tom's strong suit was baseball and since Colorado didn't have a baseball program, he went to the University of Northern Colorado. Twice he went out for the team and twice he got cut, but he got his degree and now is coaching football and two other sports—and teaching—at Burbank Junior High in Boulder. So it appears we'll have McCartney's in coaching for a long time to come.

Marc is a big, strapping kid who is a guard on Boulder High's football team and a pretty good pitcher in baseball. Marc, like all our children, has done good work in the classroom, too.

Kristy now has a schedule that would stagger even a college coach. In addition to being back at the university and working toward her degree, she's working three part-time jobs. She's a devoted mother, and between Kristy and Lyndi, they see to it that little Timothy Chase gets plenty of love and attention.

We've been fortunate with our youngsters. They accepted Jesus Christ into their lives at early ages, and are each grounded in a solid faith.

Lyndi McCartney:

In the past, I told whoever would listen that I thought all athletes and all coaches were just plain jerks. I thought the jock culture was filled with immature men so full of themselves and taken by their own importance that they were actually sub-human beings. And indeed, some of them are!

But for the most part, they're like everyone else. They have to deal with so much more than the average person ever knows. Being in the public eye isn't always as glamorous as it seems. The spotlight that shines so brightly sometimes causes temporary blindness for the athlete.

I've seen my own sons work through their own hopes and dreams and suffer their own disappointments, and what really counts is what they are as human beings; what they become after they're no longer playing children's games.

I'm deliriously happy with what our four children are as people, when the spotlight no longer shines on them.

We had our choice on enrolling the older boys at either Boulder or Fairview High Schools. We chose Boulder, even though it was obvious that Mike would have an uphill struggle on the football team: the starting quarterback, a very talented Tom Gebhardt, was not only a senior but captain of the team. But what influenced our decision was that the coach at Boulder High, Dennis Dee, was a strong Christian. We wanted that kind of influence for our boys. This wasn't merely a parental decision; the boys wanted to play for a Christian, too.

Mike didn't get to start, but in the big game of the year against crosstown rival Fairview High, Mike got into the game in the fourth quarter and led his team down the field to a touchdown. Boulder High won the game, so each of our older sons had a wonderful moment of personal achievement.

They had silenced the high expectations that had met them at the city limits. Each boy had carved his own niche. Each had proven himself beyond a shadow of doubt to the Boulder community.

Now it was my turn.

When I knew the Colorado job was mine, I had been upbeat, positive and optimistic. It didn't matter that Colorado had been losing, that attendance was down, that fans were disgruntled, that high school coaches around the state felt alienated.

I also knew why I'd gotten the job: Michigan and Bo.

And that kind of heritage had created heavy expectations in Boulder.

What Colorado people had to realize was that they were getting McCartney, not Schembechler. "I'm not Bo," I told everyone within earshot. "Anyone who leaves the Michigan program and tries to be Bo is making a grave mistake."

Even Bo assured Buff fans when we sat down at the Denver airport that I'd produce a winner. At the same time, he cautioned that it would take time.

I read once that someone had described patience as a virtue only for those who have nothing to anticipate. Football fans— whether in the Rockies or in Alabama—don't want to wait too long for a winner.

The Colorado program needed pizzazz, some excitement right away to rejuvenate the fans—and they might have gotten it quicker had Crowder selected a good offensive coach. But when he hired me, he hired a guy who had been steeped in the Michigan tradi- tion: Strong defense, ball control, good kicking game, heavy em- phasis on running. I really didn't have the base to come in and install an offense that was right for Colorado. I know LaVell Edwards of Brigham Young was one of the guys Eddie had talked with about coming to Colorado, but at BYU they'd just made a big stadium addition and it would have been a terrible time for Edwards to leave. Had Colorado gone to an interim coaching sit- uation for one year, I'm certain Edwards would have been Crowder's guy.

By the time I figured out my biggest mistakes—and was pre- pared to admit them to myself and my staff—Colorado fans were at the point where they didn't want to hear the term "rebuilding process." But a rebuilding process—and long term, at that—was exactly was it was going to take to turn the Buffaloes around.

For one thing, I knew we needed to deepen our talent, partic- ularly on defense.

On the collegiate level, the biggest discrepancy between teams is in the defensive line. Your front five allow you to control most games. If the other guy's offensive line is a lot more talented than your defensive line, they'll blow you off the football field, and you have no chance to win no matter what kind of defense you decide to play. You can be as cute and tricky as you want, but the first thing you must do in order to win is to attract the quality athletes who are big and strong and who have the maneuverability to ad- just to various styles of play.

Each year, a handful of those young men come out of high

school with all the obvious characteristics—as Jake Gaither used to say, he liked 'em agile, mobile and hostile. In the past, those players have gone to the Southern Cals, the Oklahomas, Nebraskas, Michigans, the Ohio States, the Notre Dames. The rest of the universities take the undersized kid. He may have the frame and the capacity to put on some size, but while you're waiting for him to mature, the powerhouse programs have stockpiles of talent on the defensive side. As they move new talent into the defensive lineup, the first players move over to offense and end up being extremely talented offensive linemen. Having been recruited originally as defensive players, they obviously have more speed and mobility.

When I took the job at Colorado, the program didn't have enough good football players. It was as simple as that.

Of course, there is one problem unique to the Colorado program: the state has good high school football but not enough of it. So we have to go eight hundred or a thousand miles, often a lot more, for our recruits. Scores of Big Ten coaches have said, "Give me the state of Ohio all to myself and let me have the players I want from there, and you can have the rest of the nation." That same thing could also be said for Florida, California, Pennsylvania, Texas, Georgia, Michigan, Illinois and maybe one or two more states. Which is why these states are so heavily recruited by all the solid programs in their areas, and for most of them, it means a lot fewer miles than we at Colorado have to travel.

But no matter how aggressively you recruit, regardless of how many hours you invest, you cannot be successful until you figure out which way your program is going. . .until you make firm decisions. . .until you make a commitment. And I had to stumble and fall a couple of times before I screwed up the courage to confess to my own inadequacies. I had learned a lot from Bo Schembechler and Tony Versaci, but I didn't get half-smart until I found out I didn't know it all.

It was a time of growth for everyone involved: While it's true that Colorado didn't have enough good players, they didn't have a good enough coach either—not until we began to learn together.

It was going to take a little longer than I had hoped for me to carve my niche in Boulder.

Eddie Crowder:

There were three people considered for the job, three people interviewed, all strong and capable coaches.

Chuck Shelton had come to the forefront because his team had beaten Colorado twice, and since Drake has no business beating Colorado under any circumstances, I had to be impressed by the job he was doing there.

I also talked with LaVell Edwards, but the timing wasn't right for him to leave Brigham Young.

And then there was Bill McCartney. This fellow Versaci had called and his message just jumped out at me from this huge stack of calls I'd received. I called him and we talked a long while and it's true, he gave me more background than the CIA would have required. It sounded to me like McCartney was a guy who was right on the threshold of readiness to be a successful, major college coach. Bo gave him the strongest possible recommendation, so we arranged for him to visit us.

I was immediately taken with this guy as being a quality person. He had an attractive personality, he was physically attractive, he had that strength of personality and presence—and most importantly, he had a sincerity and humility about him that made him very appealing.

One afternoon Dr. Arnold Weber, a strong leader and at that time president of the school, told me he'd expect my recommendation the following noon. Weber was a little surprised when I suggested McCartney.

(Continued)

We both liked Shelton's eagerness and we felt he was even more, well, what I'd call "immediately ready" to come in and do a job for us.

But I felt Coach McCartney, while he probably wouldn't be as effective in the early going, had the qualities to grow into the job and would be better for us in the long run. I say this without taking a thing away from Chuck Shelton, who's a fine man and a dandy coach.

You see, it's my belief that to succeed at anything, with top level performance and competition, you need to have the extra dimension I call "pedigree." And pedigree, for a football coach, means that the guy ideally should come from a top-level program with top-level competition, he needs to have played in an excellent program that was a national contender, and he needs to have coached in that same environment.

And McCartney had all that. He had played in a solid program at Missouri, he had coached at Michigan, and besides that, he had great human qualities. I felt he gave us predictability, reliability and stability. And while I was around there, we had a wonderful relationship. I'm so thrilled for him that his teams have progressed so far. It's a cliché, but really, it couldn't have happened to a nicer man.

No one can ever understand the pressures and agonies that beset a coach of a major league college football team. You know I got out at a pretty early age. I was thirty-one when I got the Colorado job and forty-two when I left it. Everyone wanted to know why I got out at such a relatively young age. Well, when coaches tell you that it's a young man's business,

(Continued)

they know what they're talking about. The harshness of the public's judgment of a coach was not something I found appealing.

One week, you get a standing ovation for breaking Joe Paterno's thirty-game undefeated streak, and the next week the same fans are upset with you because you didn't cover the point spread. It's too much of an emotional rollar coaster.

And there's no escaping it. You can be on the golf course in July, and some guy wants to talk about some play the previous October, wondering why you ran off tackle instead of throwing to the tight end. It's unreal!

That fishbowl existence grinds on a fellow. And the more success you have, the more it grinds. What Bill McCartney has endured is amazing. He's had the overwhelming task of taking a program and rebuilding it, and getting it to the place where it's getting prime national attention and playing for the national championship. Add to that the incredible personal and very painful experiences under which he's had to labor—let's just say that only a man of Bill's character and integrity could have survived.

Ten

Tradition isn't Always Married to Excellence

J ust as winning begets winning, so does losing become a downward spiral. Successful programs attract blue-chip performers. Champions breed champions. But when you have no real tradition of success, it's a titanic struggle to convince young men they're capable of winning. Not just winning more than you lose, but winning the big games; the critical games. The line between moderate success and consistently high performance may seem small, but in every conference there's that long list of the have-nots and a very small list of the haves.

Colorado had played ninety-two seasons of football before I got to Boulder. Nineteen coaches had preceded me and only four of them lasted more than five years. One of them, Frederick Folsom, was so successful and revered back at the turn of the century that they named the football field after him. Eddie Crowder, the athletic director who hired me, coached for eleven seasons and you couldn't question his coaching skills. His teams won fifty-seven per cent of their games, but beat Oklahoma only four times and Nebraska just once. And the Buffaloes of the Crowder years, although they went to five bowl games in a six-year period, never had the honor of playing in a January 1 game. And no matter how you slice it, that's the standard by which the truly outstanding programs are judged. When you play on New Year's Day, that means you have taken your football program to another level.

The man Eddie picked to take his place, Bill Mallory, coached five seasons and briefly had the Buffaloes sort of peeking in at the top level. Mallory's teams won sixty-two per cent of their games and got a piece of the Big Eight championship along with Oklahoma and Oklahoma State in 1976, as well as the Orange Bowl bid in 1977 (the final score was Ohio State 27, Colorado 10). But Mallory was 1-9 against the Sooners and the Cornhuskers.

Bill Mallory had a stormy relationship with members of the press. His critics said he was aloof and distanced himself from the media. He also didn't have the support of two of Colorado's biggest boosters, the late Bob Six of Continental Airlines and oil and land baron Jack Vickers. Mallory was fired the Tuesday after the 1978 season drew to a close. His team had started with five victories in a row and finished with three straight defeats.

Chuck Fairbanks, who'd been successful as coach at Oklahoma a few years before, was hired to replace Mallory. The experience was a disaster for the state of Colorado, the university, its football program and, I'm sure, for Fairbanks. His teams won only seven games in three years, lost six times to the big fellows and were outscored by Oklahoma and Nebraska by the combined margin of 322 to 83. In Fairbanks' last season in 1981, Oklahoma beat Colorado 49-0 and Nebraska shut out the Buffaloes 59-0.

And I went to Colorado brimming with confidence!

Fairbanks had made a sudden departure June 1 to take the job of coaching the New Jersey Generals of the United States Football

League and by the time my feet hit the ground, I had ninety-four days to line up a football team in the opening game against California.

I interviewed the leftover staff and they were very encouraging about the talent Fairbanks had left behind. They were certain we'd be a representative team, one that could be a contender with a break here and there. I kept one coach, Buck Nystrom. He had a tremendous background, having had a distinguished playing career at Michigan State where he won not only all-America honors but scholastic honors as well. And he'd coached under Fairbanks at Oklahoma and Colorado, he'd coached at Northern Michigan, North Dakota State and some twenty years before, he'd done another three-year stint on the Colorado staff.

It takes a long time, toil and good fortune to assemble an effective staff. It takes an absolute genius to hire a good staff fast—and, unfortunately, no one has accused me of having any of the characteristics one normally associates with a genius.

What we did was scramble. I kept Nystrom and a graduate assistant, and we were off and running—but not running very well. What we really did was stumble.

Two days after I was hired, two players were caught smoking marijuana so they were out. One starting offensive tackle flunked out, the other starting tackle decided he didn't want to play football any longer.

It was a sobering, almost shuddering experience when the players reported.

We gathered in a field that was about the length of a couple of football fields, and I asked our guys to run four laps. At least ten guys just plain pooped out. And the rest of them weren't running with any zeal. Colorado had no strength and conditioning coach, and I could see then and there that, for the most part, the players had insufficient strength and precious little conditioning.

Only a handful of guys were really good players who reported in top shape. Most of the others were fat, they had no muscle tone and worse, they had no pride. I'd come from a program where, almost without exception, the players had immense pride and reported in good condition. If I were to be criticized for comparing the Colorado program with what I had left behind in Michigan, so be it. What better standard to use?

I came down pretty hard that day. I said what I'd just seen was a "disgrace to college football."

Because a concert was scheduled for our stadium, we had to shift some of our practices to a junior high school field. There, a terrific lineman named Junior Ili, who later would serve as the captain of our team, broke his ankle. Our equipment was outdated, much of it was in poor shape, and anyone with any real feel for what a solid program was like could see that our battle would be an uphill one. We had seventy-three bodies and most of them weren't big enough, strong enough or fast enough to cope with what lay ahead.

I had been in town only a few weeks but I knew already what it must be like for a kitten, facing the real world for the first time with its eyes wide open. Bo Schembechler had come as far as Denver with me—he was on his way to a speaking engagement in Aspen and we took the same plane West—and he had spoken about me in confident terms to reporters at the Denver airport. He assured everyone I was "ready" for this assignment, that fans would see immediate results.

But now I knew better. I was thankful I hadn't made any outlandish promises. Instead, I had told the gathering at the airport:

"I promise you we will have a program built on integrity, honesty, character. Our top priority will be the graduation of the student athlete. That's how you're going to measure us. That's not going to be as glamorous as that scoreboard in the end zone. Maybe they won't keep a tally as pronounced. And yet, that's how we're going to measure success here."

I'm quite sure that wasn't what disgruntled Buffalo fans wanted to hear, but that's the only promise I made. Dr. Arnold Weber, CU president then and a man for whom I have abundant respect, was strong in his support of such a stand:

"Coach, there are three things you need to understand as you take over this job," he had told me. "Number one, I want an honest program. Number two, I want you to graduate your players. Three, I want you to become competitive so we can be a respectable football team."

If our players were under-equipped to compete against the likes of Nebraska and Oklahoma, they were no worse off than the football program's image within the state of California. We soon learned that many of the high school coaches were less than enamored with CU Football.

And so began the rebuilding process *beyond* the playing field. I knew I had to mend fences all over Colorado, and Lyndi accepted the fact that for a long time, most of my evening meals would be in banquet halls, church basements or roadside diners. Even though Lyndi and I knew that the first couple years in Boulder would be non-stop, that understanding didn't lessen the burden placed on Lyndi's shoulders. The responsibilities of settling into a totally new environment, putting down roots, getting the kids situated in new schools with new friends—it all fell to her.

Luckily, before long we were seeing some fruit from her great sacrifice and my hard work. The headlines in the newspapers around the country were gracious and optimistic:

Fences Mended:
McCartney has Coaches Beaming

McCartney Plans to be Visible

Optimism Flourishes in Boulder

Forget the Past Record!
McCartney Thinks "Win"

"Win" was an understatement. I was thinking more than "win"! From the moment I arrived in Boulder, I had identified Nebraska as the team we'd most like to beat. Remember, I had come off those tremendous games involving Michigan and Ohio State—now *that's* a rivalry. But when I got to Colorado and asked people which team Colorado pointed toward—which team presented the hottest rivalry and the greatest goal—I got some "Nebraska" answers and some "Oklahoma" answers and a whole lot of blank stares. Other people said frankly that it would be foolish to point for either team.

"You have to be kidding me!" I exclaimed. "You mean that's the prevailing attitude around here?"

I finally got several people to explain that they really did "hate" Nebraska more than any other opponent because their fans come by the thousands when the game in played in Boulder. Since Nebraska home games are always sold out—and Colorado's are not—Nebraska fans who can't get a ticket to see games in Lincoln eagerly make the six-hundred-mile trek to watch the Cornhuskers play at Colorado.

In my very first meeting with the players, I rattled on for half an hour about how this team—the one in the room right that moment—was going to beat Nebraska and do it right now! This year! Down through the years, we'd been competitive from time to time. Not in recent years, no, but I was hopeful that if the players checked the record books against Nebraska, they'd start from the beginning, stopping at 1961 when the rivalry was twenty years old and Colorado had a 10-9-1 edge. For in the twenty years since then, Colorado had won only one game—in 1967.

"No one will wear red around here," I told them. "We don't wear red at Colorado. And it's not just because of Nebraska—Oklahoma wears red, too. I don't want to see a red tie. And no red cars. Not even among our staff. I'm telling you, you guys can beat Nebraska."

There was only one place red was allowed: when we printed our football schedules on posters, we circled Nebraska in red.

Lyndi McCartney:

I've always believed that when you're a coach's wife, maintaining balance really is the job of the woman of the home. But instead of looking at it as merely a job, I think of it as a gift from God.

Of course, I haven't always been good at my job. I've sometimes grumbled loudly through the years. I've been frustrated, angry, resentful at times. I've played the role of the martyr—I've had the "poor me" syndrome and felt neglected and rejected.

I read somewhere that men have a bank of twelve thousand words a day and women have a bank of twenty-five thousand words a day. Bill spends most of his at work and I guess I feel like there are precious few words left in him when he gets home to me and the children. On the other hand, I spend just a few of my words during the day, and thus I have thousands left for Bill when he hits the door. Lots of times he doesn't want them.

So, I now have a savings account of hundreds of thousands of words, and if I have to use them up before I die, someone's ears are in for a lot of trouble.

We've had our hurts and struggles. Bill has always believed it's better to focus on the solutions rather than the problems—but I've managed to work up a good case of self-pity now and then. You see, I love to talk things through to a slow solution so I can thoroughly enjoy my pain!

Still, even a beautiful rose has some thorns, and I feel very fortunate because love has always been the real foundation of our family life.

(Continued)

A coach's schedule is very demanding, and it's taken me almost all the years of our marriage to understand that. Even though I understood from the start that I would have to be a stabilizing force and cornerstone of our family, there have been tough days, fighting off feelings of defeat and futility.

Let me assure you of this: I could never have maintained the balance in my home without my faith in God!

God has always been with me—but I haven't always been with God. For a time, my walk with the Lord was unsteady and faltering. But in the last two years, Jesus and I have become inseparable. I don't know why it takes so long sometimes to learn the Lord's way, and to understand that His is the only way. For so long I had my own dreams and my own fantasies—and life's realities didn't even begin to come close to them!

But finally, I am at peace with God, with myself, my husband and my children. That's not to say that I couldn't fire up a little hysteria over something inconsequential if I had to, but there's a lot less turmoil inside of me.

And best of all, I have an Anchor to quiet my soul when the world gets turbulent. I have a husband I will love until I die, and the security of knowing that he loves me in the same way. I have four children who are wonderful people—I respect and admire each one of them. I have family—mine and Bill's—that I treasure. I have friends who know my faults and love me still. I have acquantainces—and even strangers—who reach out to me in love and who pray for me. Most of all, I have the Lord in my life, a Savior who loved me when I was unworthy and unlovely.

Talking about beating the Nebraskas and the Oklahomas is one thing, but I had pulled no punches when Dr. Weber and some others asked me how long it'd take Colorado to get competitive with the "Big Two."My answer was "Seven to ten years." It wasn't what anybody wanted to hear, and it wasn't what I wanted to say but it was the truth.

Still, I had to instill a positive attitude among the players. And a good place to start was the opening game against California.

We had 17,000 empty seats and 35,103 fans at Folsom Field. Before the crowd had a chance to get settled, we had turned the ball over three times. In the first quarter alone, we suffered through four fumbles, an interception and six penalties. Cal raced out to a 21-0 lead. Just before the half, our punter was standing in our end zone, bobbled the snap and ran it out only to the eight-yard-line.In the fourth quarter we were within one touchdown and had a chance to win the game, but California closed the game with a 31-17 victory.

Saying it was an inauspicious debut doesn't quite describe it.

A week later, tables turned as we beat Washington State 12-0, marking the first time in three years a Colorado football team had won a road game.

Our third game left us hurting again. At Colorado, losing to Wyoming is unacceptable—yet we did it. And we did it at home. Only once in twenty-two games had a Colorado football team lost to this neighboring state, but we did it in grand style. Wyoming turned the ball over to us seven times and we got overwhelmed, both in the playing and the coaching departments. The loss to the Cowboys illustrated better than any other factor just where our program was in terms of quality. After a 34-6 loss to UCLA the following week, could anyone have expected us to be remotely competitive against Nebraska in week five?

Things were slipping, fast. I made a direct appeal to the very manhood of the Colorado players.

The year before, I'd been one of the speakers at Nebraska's football clinic. George Darlington, a pal of mine who's an assistant

coach for the Huskers, had invited me and during our time together, we talked about the Colorado coaching job and the football
program there.

"Colorado is intimidated by Nebraska," George had told me.
"Every time we play them, they just lay down for us."

I doubt he could have been more blunt.

Of course, neither of us had an inkling that he was talking to
the next Colorado coach, but I made certain his words got to our
players. When the squad assembled to begin preparation for Nebraska, I repeated what Darlington had told me. "This is what they
think of you," I admitted.

A lot of these young men had played against Nebraska, and for
those who had not, they could read the scores of the last four
games between the two teams:

1981: Nebraska 59, Colorado 0

1980: Nebraska 45, Colorado 7

1979: Nebraska 38, Colorado 10

1978: Nebraska 52, Colorado 14

We did everything we could to get the players and the student
body riled up. We toured sorority and fraternity houses, held a pep
rally, staged a "corn roast" and even had T-shirts made up in anticipation of victory.

When the game was history, Nebraska newspapers had fun
writing their headlines:

McCartney Finds Out it Takes

More Than Posters to Beat Nebraska

So, we didn't win the game. But entering the fourth quarter, we trailed 20-14. Someone reading the 40-14 final score in Sunday's newspaper and thinking it was a rollover would have been seriously misled. We were in it until the late, going against a Cornhusker team that had Roger Craig, Turner Gill, Mike Rozier, Irving Fryar and Dave Rimington in the lineup. The people of Colorado were proud of the way their kids played. A writer in Lincoln, Nebraska wrote in his game story:

> McCartney wants to be a winner in the worst way. He wants his players to be winners, also. His face after the game showed this. He seemed down, but there was a glimmer of hope still left in his eyes. In a few years, McCartney will be a winner as a football coach. Right now, he is a winner as a person because of the way he is trying to instill a winning attitude into his players.

Nice words, but we were still 1-4.

From the Denver Post:

New University of Colorado football coach McCartney hasn't wasted any time patching up CU's strained relations with high school coaches or making inroads into what may be the state's deepest senior crop in years.

In sharp contrast to predecessor Chuck Fairbanks, whose aloofness riled some high school coaches, Bill jumped at the chance to speak at the recent Colorado High School Coaches' Association Hall of Fame banquet.

He remained attentive through the sometimes tedious affair, laughed at the usual jokes and told the coaches they sit as a jury on the promises he's made. Then he stood as a one-man receiving line, greeting some coaches he had met at the five clinics he organized with his staff.

(Continued)

Writers wrote and sportscasters spoke of our heart, our refusal to give up. Players talked about closing the gap between the haves and the have nots, and how we'd won the respect of the Nebraska players and fans.

But we didn't win another game until the next to last week of the season, 28-3 over Kansas. And the Jayhawks won the same number of games we did that long season.

By the time we went to Lincoln for a return match the following October, we still weren't much of a team and it was my fault. Sure, we were overmatched. Until recently, for the most part when we played top teams, we were sending boys out against men. Emotion will get you by for awhile, but eventually talent will prevail if there's much of a discrepancy in the abilities of the competing teams. I came to Colorado as a defense-oriented coach and I didn't nail down any solid offensive plan for several years. I fiddled around and experimented and tried to get by with trickery to make up for our lack of ability. I vacillated and wavered and was guilty of gross indecision—the worse thing a head coach can do.

I should have brought in a top offensive coordinator, let him alone, let him install his program and stayed out of it. But I didn't. I experimented. Because of my uncertainty, I interfered. To be sure, the timing of my appointment was as terrible for the program as it was terrific for my career. I didn't have the benefit of spring football. I had missed an entire season of recruiting. First season out of the gate, I tried to do most of the things Colorado had been doing and mix in some other schemes. In 1983, we tried to develop the same system, make it smoother.

We named Ron Taylor offensive coordinator. A former quarterback for Missouri who had taken our Tiger team to a couple of Orange Bowls, Ron had a good background and was a capable guy—and he understood what we wanted to do with the Buffaloes.

But that didn't satisfy me. Sure, we moved the ball and we had our moments. . . but as I look back on it all with the advantage of hindsight, well, there were a lot of mistakes on my part. As the head coach, I just made some lousy decisions and sometimes fiddled around long enough so there was only indecision.

The truth is, I had not provided our players with enough solid leadership and direction—and here we were in late October of my second season, trying to get ready for the rival we were learning to hate.

We'd played fairly well against Michigan State and lost by six; beat Colorado State handily; manhandled Oregon State 38-14; collapsed against Notre Dame 27-3; got mauled by Missouri 59-20,and lost to Iowa State 22-10 and then had to line up against Nebraska. Naturally, the Huskers were among the top-rankedteams in the nation—and to make matters worse, the game would be played in Lincoln.

On the eve of the game, I was in my hotel room and I flicked on the television set just in time to catch Bob Devaney's show. Bob was the architect of the Nebraska dynasty, had coached the

In the years Fairbanks attended the function, he seemed rather bored as coaches exchanged tales of how he ignored their programs. . . .A CU insider said, "It took these guys six weeks to do what the old staff did in three years."

Huskers to three Big Eight titles and two national championships, and now he was athletic director. Each week, he'd talk about the conference and predict the outcome of the various games. When it came time to talk about our game the next day, the host mentioned that I had singled out Nebraska as the team Colorado would most like to beat.

"Yeah," Devaney sort of growled as a condescending smirk crossed his face. "I know that. That young coach, McCartney. . .in my opinion, he'd be a lot smarter if he pointed for Kansas State."

I'm a great admirer of Bob Devaney and it didn't offend me at all that he said what he said, nor was it an unfair thing to say. After all, Nebraska had whipped Colorado fifteen straight times and twenty of the last twenty-one meetings. You didn't have to be nearly as bright as Devaney to figure out that we didn't belong on the same field with Nebraska.

But for half a football game, we played those Cornhuskers off their feet! We trailed at the half 14-12. We had the ball for more than eighteen of the thirty minutes—although I confess we

> **People have asked me if, during those early years, we recruited athletes who had great ability but were morally corrupt. The answer is an emphatic 'No!' That's not to say we didn't take a chance on some kids. But in the long run, you don't win with bandit-athletes.**
>
> *Bill McCartney*

didn't always know what to do with it when we had it—and we had already proved a point.

Good thing, too!

Nebraska put forty-eight (count 'em: f o r t y - e i g h t) points on the scoreboard in the third quarter! Irving Fryar went for 54, Mike Rozier went for 13, Turner Gill went for 17, then hit Fryar for 34, and then Rozier went for 18 and Smith for a dozen, all of them touchdowns. Nebraska had proven a point—but then, so had we.

We were beaten but not humiliated. We were defeated but not dejected. We were overwhelmed but not overcome.

One of the real pluses that the game produced was among our red-shirt freshmen who had made the trip to Lincoln and watched from the sidelines. They saw the excitement and the intensity that our players demonstrated. They saw the effort, the caring about each other. All of us understood that the Nebraskas of college football are never going to come down to our level, and that we had to struggle and persevere and make it to theirs. And everyone now understood, I think, that selecting one opponent as your main rival and pointing to a particular game—these things are important to the team, to the fans, to the community.

We split our last four games of 1983 and wound up with a 4-7 record.

As we began to prepare for the 1984 season, I honestly felt we would begin to see significant progress. But if the 1982 and 1983 seasons had been the Andrea Doria and the Stockholm, then 1984 was the Lisitania, the Titanic and Little Big Horn all wrapped into one.

Eleven

Ed Reinhardt:
Profile of a Winner

I n our opening game of the 1984 season, we blew a last minute chance to beat Michigan State.

Still, considering that we were playing with kids who really were first-year players in our program, I was optimistic about the future. Our talent might have been green, but I knew it would ripen. Ed Reinhardt, for example—a good-looking sophomore tight-end who was one of just three players who had lettered as a freshman—caught ten passes for 142 yards and two touchdowns in that opening game against Michigan.

The following Saturday, Ed caught four passes when we played Oregon at Eugene, and one reception was for a two-point conversion that gave us the lead 20-17 in the fourth quarter. We were driving late in the game when our quarterback hit Reinhardt over the middle for a quick gain, and Ed was tackled by two Oregon players. I've seen every angle of every film taken of the hit, and to me it appeared to be a routine hit. A hard tackle, but a clean one.

"I saw the hit," Dr. Peter Ewing, one of the team doctors, told me later. "I got to him on the field and he was alert and tried to stand up. I told him not to, but he got up and more or less went off the field on his own."

Ed got up, sort of stumbled and started off the field. It appeared he then got a little groggy. He came off the field and I didn't think any more about it then.

A neurosurgeon sitting in the stands had been watching, and I'm told that when Ed started off the field, the neurosurgeon got out of his seat and headed for our bench. As it turned out, when Eddie sat down on the bench, he complained to one of his teammates about an "impossible headache."

Then he crumpled to the ground.

To my dying day, I'll be assured it was only by divine intervention that Ed Reinhardt's life was spared. The neurosurgeon who rushed to the field from the stands was Dr. Arthur Hockey. While still at the stadium, Ed was given emergency treatment, an intravenous dose of Mannitol, which, according to Dr. Julian Hoff, chief of neurosurgery at University of Michigan Hospitals, is an emergency drug used in trauma cases to shrink the bulk of brain tissue, thus reducing pressure inside the skull.

Within minutes, Reinhardt was rushed to the hospital.

There, Dr. Hockey and a team of assistants removed a blood clot from the surface of the left side of Ed's face. Later that night, the doctor told the media, "His prognosis is uncertain. He could still not survive."

Ed suffered the hit with 1:53 left in the game.

We delayed the team's departure for Boulder and I raced for the hospital. Some of us knelt in a hospital hallway to pray for Ed and his family.

Ed's mother, Pat, was in Lincoln, Nebraska, watching an older son, John, playing for the Cornhuskers. When Coach Tom Osborne heard the news, he arranged for a private jet to fly Mrs. Reinhardt to Eugene. Someone reached Ed's father, Ed Sr., back home in Denver and he, too, raced to Ed's bedside.

Years from now, when the history of the University of Colorado football program is written, it may be said of Ed Reinhardt that he had a greater impact and made a more significant contribution than any other human being.

I am persuaded that even if I live as long as I want to, I'll never meet a more courageous man nor encounter a human being with greater heart and spirit. And for all of my days, I will carry vivid memories of the vigil we maintained in that hospital in Eugene, Oregon in September of 1984.

What developed there in Eugene was one of the most loving and courageous rallies I've ever seen one family make. I doubt I'll ever see a better example of so many things coming together for good: family love and unity; everyone supporting everyone else; putting selfish interests aside for the life of one beautiful young man; demonstrating great poise and resilience. And then there were the people of Eugene and the people at the University of Oregon, too. They reached out as if Ed Reinhardt were just as special to them.

As I knelt and prayed in the hospital corridor, I remembered how I'd gone to the Reinhardt home to recruit Ed, and how he and a handful of teammates had committed themselves, wholeheartedly and with great spirit, to Colorado football at a time when everyone else still seemed to be wearing a smirk.

I've known few young men with more potential to achieve true greatness, on the field and off, as Ed Reinhardt. He was a three-sport star at Heritage High School in Littleton, Colorado. He was a top scholar-athlete and was sought by scores of colleges and universities, even though he was hurt during much of his senior year.

Ed's senior year in high school was my first year coaching at Colorado. We were determined to do a good job of recruiting the top talent in the State of Colorado, but the program had hit on hard times and it was a mighty struggle. Quality performers are naturally attracted to winning programs and while the Oklahomas and Nebraskas could offer high school stars the opportunity to join a "made" program, all we could do was appeal to in-state loyalty to come and help us build one.

I've pointed out before that since I was hired on June 10, and didn't secure a full coaching staff until July, there was no chance to do any spring or summer recruiting that first year. I had no right to think that a 2-8-1 record in our first season was going to do much to inspire young talent to come our way.

But somehow, we managed to gather a nucleus of quality young people who would, in reality, bring about the turn-around in Colorado's football fortunes. It didn't happen quickly, and with a different administration, I might have been out of there by the time it all fell into place.

We had a large group of in-state recruits on campus on the first weekend in February of 1983—we had targeted this date for in-state recruiting. These fine young men got together as a group, took a hard look at a program that had produced only nine victories in four seasons, and decided to come to Boulder. These were good kids, sharp kids with a lot going for them. Eddie Reinhardt told us at midnight on the eve of the signing date that he'd decided to come to Colorado. Curt Koch, a defensive tackle from Littleton, jumped on board one day later. Jon Embree of Englewood, an all-starter at tight end, joined the group as did David Tate, a receiver from Denver. Sam Smith, a fine running back from Aurora, got on board along with an outstanding punter, Barry Helton of Simla. The player we most wanted was Eric McCarty, a running back in our back yard at Boulder.

Whenever my coaching days are over, and whether I ever have another opportunity to play for a national championship, I will have a special place in my heart for this group of young men who got on board a ship others believed was floundering, and helped steer it out of stormy waters. It was local talent that initially brought Colorado football out of the dark times. And talk about quality young men!

McCarty was picked as the top scholar-athlete in the state, and could have gone to Michigan, Stanford, Southern Cal or almost anywhere else in the land. And he had a 3.7 grade point average. Today, he's in medical school and you can count on Eric McCarty one day being a fine physician.

Embree lettered in three sports, worked hard at Colorado and got his degree and performed with exceptional skills on the field—good enough to play in the National Football League for the Los Angeles Rams. And he picked Colorado even though he was being courted by Ohio State, UCLA and Southern California.

Koch was a six feet, seven inch stringbean kid of 215 pounds, who filled out to 270 in college. After he'd gotten good enough to become a pre-season all-

The Reinhardts, Ed Sr. and Pat, have six children: John, Rosemarie, Ed Jr., Tom, Paul and Mathew. They talked about their son, Ed, his decision to go to Colorado, the injury and the rehabilitation struggle:

Pat Reinhardt: I think what really turned Ed around was the weekend they had for the players from the state of Colorado. They had set it up so it would be the last recruiting visit on the boys' schedules. At that time, several of the young Colorado men got together after dinner—they were staying at the same place—and they simply decided they all wanted to be a part of turning the Colorado program around. In essence, they made their own decisions.

Other schools, particularly Stanford, were working very hard on Ed. But there was one thing that happened

(Continued)

American choice before his senior year, he and teammate Don DeLuzio were the victims in a hit-and-run accident as they walked along a Texas road during spring break. So he fought back once more and was good enough to be drafted by the Washington Redskins. Like the others, Curt was an excellent student.

Tate could have made it big in basketball as well as football and, like the others, spurned a host of other schools to join our program. And he's still getting the job done for the Chicago Bears.

Smith was a state record holder in track, won all state honors in football and started two seasons in basketball. And Sam elected to try to help build a winner, rather than join an established program. Like each of the others, he got his degree from Colorado and today he works as an executive in Phoenix, Arizona.

Helton's high school career reads like a fairy tale—A-8 player of the year three straight times, he threw for a mile and a half of yardage and 39 touchdowns as a senior, first team all state, holder of two handfuls of state passing records, three state state championships, a four-letter winner in basketball and baseball and besides all that, was valedictorian of his high school class with a perfect 4.0 grade point average! To show you my coaching genius, I turned him into a punter! He was an all-American three seasons in a row and for the past two years he has been the punter for the Super Bowl champion San Francisco 49ers.

Three other players joined that class to give us a strong in-state complement in our first campaign. They were quarterback Rick Wheeler, tight-end Troy Wolf, and place kicker Dave DeLine.

Only young men of special character could have gotten together as high school graduating seniors and made a joint decision to undertake such a task. In a sense, they sacrificed themselves, and dedicated themselves to a project that offered them little chance at personal glory. They're the ones who turned Colorado football around, and led the Buffaloes to a bowl game after the 1985 season. They were mature beyond their years and showed great loyalty to their state and, you could say, blind faith in a program that had been in a long-time tailspin.

that I believe had a tremendous influence on our son. Coach McCartney gave Ed a verse of Scripture to read. We were happy about that, because at that point we knew that Coach McCartney was a Christian.

I remember Eddie lying on the floor in the living room, looking up that verse in the Bible. Suddenly he jumped up and ran into the kitchen and asked his father where he should go to school.

Ed Reinhardt, Sr.: We didn't want to influence him. I hesitated, but I really had the conviction that he should go to Colorado. Joe Kapp was coaching California then, and I liked his free spirit. And Stanford was most impressive. But I really thought our son should be with a guy like McCartney, and since Ed had asked me a direct question, I was honest with him about the way I felt.

After the decision was made, none of us ever looked back. And we have no regrets about the decision. Later on, after the accident, Pat and I went back to CU and spoke to parents of recruits, and we told them straight out that we'd do it the same way if we had to do it over again.

Pat Reinhardt: We've always been a family of strong beliefs, but Eddie's injury has drawn all of us closer together. It's been a very hard struggle and there have been some difficult times. It's a daily, on-going walk with the Lord. Sometimes Ed moans and groans and yells, and sometimes he gets mad and frustrated, but not for long. He never gets so frustrated that he quits. He talks about wanting to coach, but of course he has some difficulty with double vision, and he can't read well or write well or type at this time. But he never gives up,

(Continued)

and neither do we, because we believe that with God, all things are possible.

From the time our children were small, we've always had Bible study before every game they ever played—football, basketball, track, whatever. There are lots of Scriptures appropriate for athletes, and they'd try to memorize them, and keep God's word close to them while they competed.

We're proud of all our children. Eddie and I went out to lunch right before he went back to college for his sophomore year—just a few months before his accident—and he was troubled that he didn't seem to be able to witness the way some of his friends could. I told him that it wasn't so much how one talked, but how one lived his life that told people how he felt about Jesus.

Since the accident, untold numbers of people have expressed to us how wonderfully Ed has witnessed to them. That's been the most comforting thing about it all—the knowledge that his life has counted for something. That even though, since his injury, Ed hasn't been able to communicate verbally the way he'd like to, that he's still living his life in a way that has a tremendous influence for good in the lives of so many people.

Ed Sr.: All this has brought about a spiritual change in me. My awareness of the Lord working through people has greatly increased. I've observed kindness and consideration that I never noticed before. It's certainly made me closer to the Lord. I can see Him working through people, and I have

(Continued)

a much better understanding of my own faith and of how God works in this world.

We nearly lost a son, but I feel that God has given us a great gift in that our son did not become bitter and angry. It's a tremendous feeling to know the impact he's had on the lives of others. Young people have come out of nowhere to our door to tell us how Eddie has helped them, and what an influence he's had on their lives.

Pat: We simply cannot give up. His therapy is practically a fulltime thing. Our first volunteers come at six-thirty in the morning and the last ones leave at nine at night. Ed only takes a two-to-three hour break between his morning and evening therapy sessions, plus an hour at dinnertime, a half-hour for lunch, and half an hour for a nap. Then, all night long he is on a machine that helps get more oxygen to his brain. The volunteers have been coming here for five years. They're really wonderful. Some of the people who have come here to help Ed have their own personal problems and trag-edies to deal with, and still, they want to help someone else. The Lord surely is at work in our lives.

When you're recruiting young men for an established program, you need not be a super salesman. But when you're not winning and you tell young men they can be part of a salvage job, you'd better aim your remarks at really special young people, quality people willing to sacrifice. Somehow, I'll always believe this group of young people sensed—even at those tender ages—that they could be part of something greater than individual glory.

And none of them have had more influence on me for good than has Ed Reinhardt.

We red-shirted most of our recruits in 1983—held them out of competition—but Reinhardt was destined to play from the very beginning. When he came back for his sophomore year, we put every player on our squad through a battery of tests to determine the best conditioned athlete on the team, and Ed missed being the top conditioned athlete by the margin of half a point. Add to that the fact that he was a marvelous student and an outstanding Christian young man, and you have every ingredient for success.

Then, in the batting of an eyelash, the future was stolen from him. The life that he and his family had every right to anticipate would be rich and rewarding was suddenly altered. And whatever plans his parents—Ed Sr. and Pat—had had for their own lives, suddenly that was altered, too. Everything went on the back burner. Suddenly nothing mattered but their commitment to their son, and they rallied around that singular cause.

All these things and more surfaced in my thoughts and prayers as I sought God in a hallway in a Eugene hospital. Doctors had removed a chunk from Ed's head, leaving a hole big enough to fit a man's fist, and I knew Ed Reinhardt was battling for his life.

There was no assurance that Ed would live as I gathered the players to prepare to play Notre Dame. When I stood up to address our young men, I found myself looking into a sea of blank faces; young men whose hearts were heavy with grief and fear. All that week, their minds were on their teammate, not on the opponent, and I couldn't blame them.

Buddy Martin of the *Denver Post* came by to see me, and he wondered about my outlook on football and the sometimes-violent nature of the sport. He wanted me to comment on the dangers inherent in the competition, and this is what I told him:

"The rewards and returns of playing football—there is almost nothing our society offers today that can make a man out of a boy and teach wholesome values of hard work and discipline and being a member of a team. All the things that youngsters have to learn—commitment, excellence, the things that make up the very fiber of our society—football teaches these things. It teaches them better than anything else that we have. I'm convinced of that. There isn't anything easy about playing football. It's the most difficult thing we do. It's not fun to practice; it's hard to practice. Practices are demanding. Taxing. Exacting. They require all of a guy. The end result is that a guy spends himself in a worthy cause. And he learns to get up off the ground, time and time again. He lines up, like some of my guys will, against somebody bigger, stronger and faster than he is. And he learns to compete. And battle. Eddie Reinhardt is doing that right now. He's drawing on all of his experiences. And he's fighting. He's got a great fighting heart. Football helped develop that in him. When a guy finishes playing football, regardless of how much he's played in terms of being in the limelight, he's a better man."

Practice that week was a blank. All of us, players and coaches, went through the motions. We had done a lot of praying for Eddie. That weekend when the team landed in South Bend for a game, I secluded myself in my motel room and began to pray some more: for Eddie and for the team, as well. I raised my hands toward

Heaven and pleaded with Almighty God to give us a blessing. I asked God to help all of us through this time of torment, and I prayed for a verse of Scripture that would give me an idea of the mind of God on all this. The one God directed me to was II Timothy, chapter two, verse three:

"You therefore must endure hardship as a good soldier of Jesus Christ."

Pardon me, Lord, but that wasn't exactly what I had in mind! Could God not have directed me toward a verse about prosperity? Psalm 98:1 would have been nice: "Oh, sing to the Lord a new song! For He has done marvelous things; His right hand and His holy arm have gained Him the victory."

I could have more readily accepted I Corinthians 15:57: "But thanks be to God, who gives us the victory through our Lord Jesus Christ."

Instead, I got a lesson in steadfastness, a new charge about strong faith in long-suffering. I asked for a gift and what God told me was simply this: "Coach, this isn't going to get any better."

The next afternoon we didn't even want to play. Even our best players—their hearts just weren't in it. We were terrible. Notre Dame could have named the score. As it was, Gerry Faust was more than merciful to hold the score to 55-14.

We didn't need any more defeats, but we got them. Ten of them. Our only victory was against Iowa State. It was a very hard year for all of us. We were improvising. We were too small, our defense couldn't get the ball back for us and we were always forced to try and come from behind. Our young offensive linemen were being beaten, and because of our inexperience, everybody was blitzing the daylights out of us. It was chaos. There were times when it looked like we didn't know what we were doing. And I'll tell you something—a lot of times we didn't.

We reached the absolute lowest point—rock bottom, in fact—in our program in the final game of 1984 when we got routed by Kansas State 38-6. The plane ride back to Boulder was the most trying of my life—but picking up the Sunday morning newspapers back home was even more deflating.

There it was: headline news. One of our players, Loy Alexander, was questioning everything about the program. He questioned the people we were recruiting, whether they were nice guy Jesus freaks who couldn't play big time football. "We have enough choir boys," he said, "and what we really need is football players." He suggested that the strongly religious player got preferential treatment, and said he wasn't the only one who suggested that I might be giving Christians more playing time.

Seven victories in three years, precisely the same number Chuck Fairbanks rang up in the three previous seasons. And when he left, one headline writer had put it this way:

End of an Error.

Anytime a new coach takes over a program—especially a faltering one—there's a certain period of grace. People hadn't judged me quickly. Even the media had been very supportive.

Bill McCartney:

When skies were darkest, that's when Lyndi came through like a champion for both me and the children. It wasn't so much what she'd say in times of great stress, but how she responded to crises. She was a solid rock, a dependable helpmate who needed only to look at me, or touch my hand, to let me know that she understood and that she would be at my side no matter what.

But in that third season, when we lost every game but one, a lot of folks were ready to jump ship and head for the lifeboats.

Not many coaches will confess to being thin-skinned and sensitive to criticism—but I say, show me someone who enjoys criticism and I'll show you someone who needs counseling! During this rough period, I had tremendous and unqualified support from

Eddie Crowder. He was encouraging, tried to offer a little wisdom here and there, and mainly tried to keep me from getting discouraged. But we both knew we were a long way from turning the corner. My, but that corner was a long way off—a lot longer than I had ever dreamed.

Before that season, Crowder decided to resign as athletic director, and I applied for his job in addition to my own. It was a mistake. I was trying to protect myself. Let's face it—if I were athletic director, I certainly wouldn't fire myself as football coach. I'd be patient and understand that building a sound and successful football program takes more than a handful of years.

The university president at the time, Arnold Weber, never took my candidacy seriously. He didn't think I could handle both jobs, and they gave the athletic directorship to Bill Marolt. Bill was a Colorado graduate and a native of the state. He'd been an outstanding skier for Colorado, coached its ski team and gone on to be an Alpine director of the U.S. Olympic ski team that did so well in the Olympic Games in Sarajevo.

Naturally, I was concerned that there might be tension between the two of us because he got the job I'd sought. But if Bill had any resentment in him, he never showed it. And when it came to my job, he said he believed in continuity, that you solve problems by sticking with people.

My, how he stuck with me! We were 0-5 at the time and, of course, there were rumors swirling about that I might not be back. Right about that time Marolt "rewarded" me with a new contract. The action drew fire from some of our fans.

All the time I was telling anyone who would listen that "We're making progress, but you just can't see it right now," and things like, "We're really coming along okay, it's just sort of hidden below the ground."

Below the ground? Right. That's where some of the Colorado fans wanted to put me.

Bill McCartney:

Several weeks ago—nearly six years after our vigil in the hospital on the day Ed was injured—Ed Reinhardt and I took part in a banquet program in Denver.

I watched and listened in absolute awe as Ed stood and sang a song. Here is a man who had every reason in the world to give up, yet he stood there—this handsome young fellow who still cannot speak in sentences—and astounded that audience by getting through the song without any words in front of him, and without missing a beat. He brought the house down.

On that night in May of 1990, I wept and at the same time I smiled, as I have done so many times before, at a remarkable display of grit. Eddie Reinhardt's story surely is one of the most tragic and at the same time one of the most inspirational stories ever told.

Today Ed spends more time each day in rigorous, yes, even torturous labor merely trying to become a whole person again, than most men do in a week of hard work. What Ed does in his determination to get well is slave labor—but he readily does it, and most of the time with a smile on his face. He's still the great competitor that he was back then.

The brain damage is such that Ed cannot speak in sentences, and yet he has this marvelous musical talent. The healing of the brain is such a slow and uncertain process, yet Ed has progressed to a point where he jogs, and he has completed a ten-kilometer run, albeit with a decided limp. He has made it known that he, one day, wants to be able to return to the university to complete work on his degree and become a

(Continued)

coach—and that only the powerful intervention of God will let that happen.

There's another former player from Ed's class who has had a profound influence on me. He was no star; in fact, he was on the squad four years and saw only spot duty on occasion. At one point, he'd been red-shirted, and even though he could have been on the squad another season, he was bitter that he hadn't gotten to play more and lashed out at me in frustration.

I met with him and gave him some choices. One of the hard things to do as a coach is to be totally—and sometimes painfully—candid with a player. I told this young man that I'd keep him on scholarship, of course, whether he came out for his final season or not. But I explained upfront that he wouldn't play much and that he'd have to improve on his attitude and rid himself of some of his bitterness. He chose not to play.

He wrote me a strong letter of criticism, and his main point was that I was a professing Christian, yet sometimes I swore on the sidelines; I was a man who proclaimed my faith in God, yet I still was able to scream and yell at my players, my staff and officials; I was a man, he said, who boasted of one lifestyle yet led another because I was unable to maintain poise and composure on the sidelines. And that, he said, was the reason he chose not to play for me. He said I was a phony, and not the man I pretended to be. I cried when I read it, because it hurt. I still have the letter, and every once in a while I read it again. And each time I read it, it hits me all over again.

(Continued)

I confess I'm not the man I want to be, and I'm not the Christian I should be or can be or hope to be—but I'm a struggling Christian who is growing and making progress; one who makes mistakes, yet wants his life to be the very best it can be before God Almighty. I've studied the Old Testament, and discovered that if a king was honorable, his people served the Lord. If the king was corrupt, his people didn't serve the Lord. The principle I see in all of that is that if the man in charge does the right things—even though he sometimes has to do the tough or unpopular thing—he nevertheless sets the direction for the program. When I read these Bible stories, I find that the people who were wholehearted for God often had to make difficult decisions.

Regardless of the success our program at Colorado may achieve, we will never have a squad of 100-plus athletes, each one absolutely delighted with his role on the team. The coaches whose achievements give them legendary status—Rockne, Bryant, Hayes, Lombardi, Landry, Schembechler, Paterno, Robinson, Warner, Stagg—must have left a trail of unhappy players behind them. Surely they agonized over the tough decisions they had to make, and they might have even made a wrong one now and again.

Before I call it quits, I'll be criticized by other players, but none will drive me to my knees faster than the young man bold enough to point out weaknesses that keep me from being the best I can be. But I'm working on it, with God's help, everyday.

And there'll never be another player who'll inspire me, lift me up, the way Ed Reinhardt does. Because of his faith in God, his unflagging attitude and his indomitable spirit, I'll be a better man tomorrow than I am today.

Twelve

The Building Blocks

If some players and fans were questioning my coaching, they weren't alone. I was questioning myself, too, wondering if I could be a good head coach, seeking answers about myself and my program. I fasted and prayed and I came out of it more determined than ever.

We made staff changes. I fired two coaches and two others quit. And yes, there was bitterness and hostility and resentment. It's difficult to make those tough decisions, because you know these men and their wives, and jobs are hard to come by in this profession. But if you are to be successful, you have to make the tough decisions. What we did, I felt, was the right thing to do. As I prayed hard about these decisions, I read the Book of James, where he advised us not to be tossed and turned by the waves.

When I found myself, and Colorado's program, on the floor

after three seasons, I resolved I would bite the bullet—but I refused to be tossed and turned by the waves that confronted me.

As we began immediate preparations for 1985, we looked around the country and pinpointed teams that had made significant turnarounds in one season. We noted that Army had beaten Michigan State in the Cherry Bowl game in Jim Young's second season. Young had done a major flip-flop and turned a losing program into a successful one. What was he doing that we could beg, borrow or steal?

Next we noted that Air Force had beaten Notre Dame four straight years and no one in his right mind would suggest that the Air Force Academy had better talent.

Finally, Jim Wacker had done wonders at Texas Christian, long one of the doormats in the Southwest Conference. He had made a run at the SWC championship and gotten the Horned Frogs into a bowl game.

These three programs had one thing in common: Option football.

When you're not good enough up front, you double-team the enemy's middle guard and leave another player unblocked. Instead of wasting your time trying to block some guy you know you can't handle, you force *him* into making the decision on who carries the ball. What he does determines whether the quarterback, the fullback or the other running back gets the ball. And by double-teaming the other monster who's way too good for your little guys up front, you generally make some kind of hole and some kind of gain, particularly if your quarterback is talented enough to make good decisions quickly after the coach has made a bad one in play selection.

Once again, I applied myself as a student of the game. I was hungry to learn.

I was even hungrier to win.

The football isn't designed to bounce true, and I've griped about bad breaks about as much as any coach alive. But the fact is, the breaks pretty much even themselves out over the course of your career.

I'll tell you what creates bad breaks in football: When your offensive line can't handle the people they're trying to block, you can get a lot of bad breaks because these monsters are coming at your quarterback and forcing him to get rid of the ball before he'd like to. When your quarterback isn't experienced and poised and instinctive, you get bad breaks. When your receivers are being belted around and they begin to hear footsteps every time they run a pattern over the middle, you can run into a lot of bad breaks.

At the beginning of the 1985 season, I knew we'd taken our share of bad breaks. And I was determined the new year would be different.

Yet, history was against us.

When you check the record books and discover that your football team has won only fourteen of its last

Don Nehlen was head football coach at Bowling Green State University, joined Bo Schembechler's staff at Michigan in 1977 before becoming head coach at West Virginia in 1980. Said Nehlen:

When I went to Michigan, Bill had been there three years and we coached on opposite sides of the football. First time I got around him I thought to myself, "This guy is almost too nice to be real."

But I soon learned that he really is a gentle, giving person and an extremely religious man. He impressed me as a man who always wanted to do what was right. He was good to the players and they believed in him, and that sincerely helped make him one of the best recruiters in the world.

After I went to West Virginia, I still went back to Michigan quite a bit, and on every visit, McCartney would grab me and we'd go to a little diner not far sixty-six games, there are lots of things working against you. For example, how could Colorado expect to persuade national recruits to come to a program that, from every outward appearance, seemed so downtrodden? Could we blame members of the press for not comprehending that we were rebuilding and that full recovery could not be expected in two, three or even four years? Could we blame fans for staying away in droves? Could I blame the critics who condemned athletic director Bill Marolt for having given a losing coach a contract extension right in the heart of a 1-10 season?

Not really. But I did. You see, I was the coach of losing teams, but I was never, ever a loser! And neither were the young people who played for those teams, because they tried very hard to win. We just couldn't get it done.

I was unaccustomed to losing. I wanted success *right now*. Losing was not then, nor is it now, an acceptable way of life for me. Had I been inclined toward an Eastern religion, believe me I would have worn out a dozen prayer rugs. Yes, I asked God to bless our program. Yes, I asked

> **Certainly a break here and there can turn a game around, but more often than not, a team that is emotionally tough and physically prepared will create its own breaks.**
>
> *Bill McCartney*

God to evangelize our players. Yes, I asked God to enlighten me and make me a better coach. Yes, I asked God to give me more discipline and control on the sidelines. Yes, I asked God to make me more perceptive to individual players' needs, to be more attentive to their complaints, their fears, their apprehensions. I did all that—and I still do—because I know that without Him, I am nothing.

One more thing. I was then, and am now, willing and even eager to recruit choir boys—provided they can play really good ball.

Don't ask me how, but I knew that going into the 1985 season, we would be a respectable football team. I sensed, and so did our staff, that we had turned the corner.

We had, after all, already turned the corner in two other areas—local recruiting and academics. It was fine that we were actively recruiting and using young men from within the state of Colorado—nice public relations gesture and it made the locals happy, although my first responsibility was to recruit football players and not goodwill ambassadors. And it was great that our program would not be an academic embarrassment to this great university, nor land us on NCAA probation.

But ninety-five percent of the people in the world judge a football coach on the number of victories his teams achieve. And they're the ones who influence the decisions about whether a coach stays or goes. It was small consolation to them that we showed good effort. An *E* for effort doesn't get it.

from the athletic offices, and he'd pump me about what I was doing at West Virginia to turn the program around, because when I took the job there, West Virginia was regarded as one of the ten worst programs in college football.

Bill never quit working, never slowed down in his quest to absorb everything he could about every aspect of the game.

Shortly after I came to West Virginia, Dr. E. Gordon Gee was elevated from dean of the law school to president of the university. A few years later, he became president at Colorado, and I told Bill he was getting a great man who'd support him in building a successful and clean program.

They're on the same page: They both want to win but they won't cheat, they care about the kids and they want them to graduate and lead successful lives when football is behind them.

The *W* is the one that matters.

No one listened when we said we had "turned the corner."

In the spring of 1985, Dick Connor wrote a nice column in the Rocky Mountain News and concluded it by saying:

> He could have compromised and shortcutted and cheated. But Bill McCartney doesn't do things that way. But only now, as his fourth year begins, do we get to start to decide whether Bill MCartney's way is the one that finally leads the Buffs out of the maze they've wandered in for a decade.

People were waiting for proof.

As we began the 1985 season, we had a new offense — the wishbone — and now we had to make it work. We had a reassembled staff—it was time to see if it could lead and direct. We had new players—and even the old ones weren't so old at that—and we needed to find out if they were a *team*. Had they listened to me, and understood, as the Michigan players had understood Bo Schembechler? Did they really understand that in order to be successful as a unit, they would have to put aside those anxious yearnings for personal glory, subjugating those whims to the good of the squad?

We had the foundation for success. Now, in 1985, it was time to build on that foundation. We needed to begin erecting *building blocks*, and I knew exactly which crucial games could provide those for us.

We beat Colorado State in the opener. It wasn't a building block, but it was an important victory—for bragging rights, as sportscasters like to say—in the state.

Then, we came from behind on "Ed Reinhardt Day" and beat Oregon. It was almost a year to the day after Ed's injury and he returned, recovered, to Boulder as we paid tribute to Ed and the people of Eugene who had been so kind and generous to both Ed and his family. The ovation for Ed that day was the most thunderous and I'm sure the most genuine I've heard.

The next week we lost to Ohio State.

We then put our first building block in place against Arizona.

This was a solid Arizona team, ranked in the top twenty. We played in Tucson. It's always tough to win on the road, and this victory proved something not just to the coaches but to the players as well. I'm persuaded that this was the moment when they really began to believe in themselves. Our defense held Arizona to sixty-four yards on the ground and our wishbone clicked for 301 yards on the ground. Again, we came from behind for the victory.

It's been said by a lot of famous coaches that inferior teams figure out ways to lose and solid teams figure out ways to win. Against Oregon, we not only had come from behind in the fourth quarter, but made a ferocious goal-line stand after Oregon had first-and-goal from our five. In three plays, Oregon had gained only two yards. A field goal wouldn't be enough to win. The Oregon quarterback, Chris Miller—so good he's still playing in the National Football League—would have beaten other Colorado teams but on the final play of the game, our Mickey Pruitt sacked him for a 14-yard loss. And against Arizona, well, there were lots of ways we could have lost, relinquishing the lead in the third quarter, but this Colorado team found a way to extract victory.

We waited only seven days to erect a second building block.

In my first three years at Colorado, the Missouri Tigers had named the score against us (35-14, 59-20, 52-7) and my staff and I were resolved to put a stop to all this nonsense. Before the season began, we had invited seventy-five former Colorado football players to return for homecoming—but we didn't tell the squad. We had set it up so that when we went on the field for our pre-game warmups, the old grads slipped into the locker room and waited for our players. On that Saturday afternoon, the pre-game pep talk belonged to the grizzled old grads.

My friends, these geezers were no choir boys!

I wouldn't have risked a show of hands on whether they all thought Bill McCartney was doing a good job coaching the Buffaloes, but they were in my corner on that October afternoon. These old guys wanted victory. They had blood in their eyes. A couple of them might even have had a little bracer before addressing the troops.

About a half-dozen of them spoke, and there was electricity in that locker room. They talked about the old days, when the Colorado teams of another era didn't take any stuff from Missouri. . .when they refused to be dumped on. . .when they returned a hard hit with a harder one. The didn't dress up their talks with a lot of cute little phrases. What they had to say, they said from their heart. There was terrific communication that day. I kept watching the players as they squirmed; the couldn't wait to get away from those guys and out of that locker room, and get after Missouri.

Yes, on that day, we had a tremendous emotional edge—but we had talent, too, and the Rocky Mountain high lasted for sixty minutes.

Final score: Colorado 38, Missouri 7.

We had an easy time of it the following week against Iowa State and suddenly Colorado was getting a taste of national attention. We had gone from among the worst teams in major college football in rushing (59.7 yards a game) to one of the best (308.3 yards per game) and people were asking if the Buffaloes were for real. I couldn't afford to be any more than cautiously optimistic because three of our final five opponents were Nebraska, Oklahoma and Oklahoma State—and frankly, I knew they were better and deeper than we were. Still, I made certain we pointed for Nebraska.

Even though we lost the game, the October 26 game against Nebraska was another building block for the Colorado team.

I read and repeated to myself—and to our players—all those deep quotes from famous men of the past: Adversity introduces a man to himself; just as the strongest steel is forged in the hottest heat, so is the greatest character forged in times of great stress; and the old chestnut, when the going gets tough, the tough get going.

Yes, we lost, against a team that came into the game ranked seventh in the nation. But consider these factors: The game was played in Lincoln, our regular quarterback Mark Hatcher was out with a broken ankle and our second string quarterback got knocked out for the season the second time he touched the ball. The young man who ended up running our offense that day was Craig Keenan, and he'd had appendicitis the previous week. We made a gallant effort and had the lead in the game, but we simply ran out of talent and gas—but never out of spiritual and enthusiasm. Nebraska beat us 17-7, but we had proved a point—if to no one else, to ourselves and I think to the doubters who cheered for the Buffaloes. We were no longer a patsy on tough teams' schedules. And at the end of that season, we went to a bowl game for the first time since the Orange Bowl of 1977.

We had pulled off the biggest turnaround in NCAA football, prompting Bill Connors to write in *College and Pro Football Newsweekly:*

> By the conclusion of this, his fourth season at Colorado, Coach Bill McCartney suddenly had a dinner. He had it, for one, because he recruited the Buffaloes out of the doom and gloom he inherited at Boulder in early 1982. Colorado's once prodigious flunkout and dropout rates dropped significantly since McCartney's recruits arrived at Colorado. And Colorado's faculty saluted McCartney for finding athletes able to meet Colorado's academic standards, which are the highest in the Big Eight Conference.

> Then Connors quoted one unnamed conference coach as saying, when he first learned I had installed the wishbone offense, "Bill's lost his mind. He's digging his grave."

Wrote Ralph Routon:

But the sweetest part of the upcoming offseason will be that McCartney won't have to make promises anymore, talking about hopes and dreams. Now he can relive a year of solid accomplishment plus many team and individual honors. He can even talk about Nebraska and Oklahoma without hearing snickers.

What Dick Connor wrote in the Rocky Mountain News harkened back to my arrival at Colorado:

He did not find an empty cupboard when he arrived in June 1982, after Chuck Fairbanks' unconscionably late defection to the USFL. It was never as simple as a restocking. He found no cupboard. He had to build one before he could pronounce it bare. There was a beautiful coach's office and little else. There was, for instance, no weight program. There were only 77 players on the roster (the NCAA allows 95 on scholarship and you can have a lot more than that as long as they're non-scholarship walk-ons), 73 on scholarship and 12 of those were junior college stopgaps.

And all this time you believed these coaches who insist they never, ever read what's written about them and never tune in to hear what sportscasters might say about them!

I met each week with two luncheon groups, the Denver Buff Club on Thursdays and the Boulder Buff Club on Fridays. In the early going, we almost could have met in a telephone booth. We've always had a handful who've been there through thick and thin, and that handful believed me, I think, when there was no evidence to support what I was saying. Jim Lassiter wrote in *The Daily Oklahoman*, "It wasn't so long ago that folks were reluctant, if not downright embarrassed, to share a meal with the CU coach. Suddenly, though, they won't leave him alone. Either at mealtime or any other time."

And I didn't want to be left alone. It was important to keep our players believing in themselves and to keep fans believing in the program.

As we prepared for the 1986 season, we had every reason to believe our program was on track and that success was just around the corner.

Suddenly, through the first four games of the 1986 season, our ears were pinned way back. We lost our opener to Colorado State, which is simply unacceptable with Buff fans. We lost the next three games—to Oregon, Ohio State and Arizona—by a total of eight points.

Two years before, one writer had predicted that I wouldn't keep my job through the 1-10 season. Now, our troubles seemed to be mounting again. It was no time for soothing talk about how close we had been in those games and how we could have won all three. The awful fact was that Colorado was 0-4.

Frankly, I thought it was the beginning of the end. Again, I was questioning my own abilities and those of our staff and players. I was numb, depressed. We're told in Scripture that we are to close the door so we are alone, where we will not be seen, and then offer our petitions to God. And I fell to my knees and prayed like a simpering child.

"Why, Lord," I pleaded, "must I go through this again? Why do I have to experience this further?"

I can't tell you how long I was in prayer, for I lost track of time, but after a while I was struck by a very clear message. God was saying to me, "Why are you acting like this? Why are you carrying on so? Why are you complaining and crying and acting like a loser instead of claiming what I have already given you?"

In my heart, I believe that strong men lead weak men. All down through history, strong men have been able to rally and incite and motivate and challenge other men to perform great deeds, to accomplish even what they feel they cannot. At that point in my career, I was being anything but strong. It was time to quit moaning and saying, "Why me, God?" and get on with the business at hand.

We had an off-week in the schedule and I called a squad meeting. The assistant coaches were on the road recruiting so there was just me and the players in that room.

When I stood before them I said: "I'm going to tell all of you something right now: Colorado is all through losing. We will win and win and win and we're not losing any more around here. We're not losers; we're winners."

There was no great flourish among the players. Not a single man volunteered to go impale himself on a dagger for me and good ol' Colorado.

Two weeks later we beat Missouri on the Tigers' home field, then we dominated Iowa State. We had boosted our record to 2-4 when we set about the business of getting ready for Nebraska. That game would be a critical building block.

Four years ago, the first time we pointed toward Nebraska, people laughed. The Colorado team of four weeks ago might have stumbled at the memory of our 20-year losing streak against the Huskers. The Bill McCartney of four weeks ago might have had his share of doubts, too. But that was before.

This was now.

We never even trailed in that game. We beat a Nebraska team that was ranked third in the country, and we held the Cornhuskers' vaunted ground game to 123 yards.

The victory meant so much to all of Colorado that we left the scoreboard lit until Monday afternoon. Not only that, we went on to beat Oklahoma State and Kansas until we stumbled and lost to third-ranked Oklahoma in our final regular season game.

What a tremendous lesson I learned from that season! The things we say to ourselves really do move us in the direction that we go. We can embrace a loser's attitude, as Teddy Roosevelt once said, and "take rank with those poor spirits who neither suffer much nor enjoy much." We can put on that hang-dog expression and assume the posture and attitude of a loser.

Or we can claim the promises of Jesus Christ. We can get into His playbook and enjoy a resurrected spirit. When I changed my attitude about Bill McCartney, I started leading like a real man for the very first time.

We were through being embarrassed against the great teams. We were now at the point where they could not look at their schedule in August and safely forecast a *W* the day they played us. We were not quite where we wanted to be, but we were gaining on 'em and our players now believed in themselves and in each other. We finally were becoming a *team* instead of a bunch of individuals.

We lost four games in 1987, to Oregon, Oklahoma State, Oklahoma and Nebraska. When we went to Norman to play Oklahoma,

---

Woody Widenhofer:

When Bill had his born-again experience, he couldn't wait to tell me about it. He's never tried to oversell it, or tried to shove it down my throat, but he sent me a book to read and he does talk about it—but more than that, he lives it. Even in the tough times.

I know he went through a tremendous valley in his early years at Colorado, and thank God he had an administration that stuck with him. Those things take time.

People on the outside don't understand what it takes, and they don't understand the pressures of this kind of job. In football, the jury deliberates every week. There isn't a professor in any college in America who is under the scrutiny a football coach lives with every day. No one evaluates a professor that way. In football, you have thousands of jurors in the stands and a lot of

(Continued)

the Sooners were ranked number one and they were the defending national champions. For as long as anyone in Colorado could remember, Oklahoma had intimidated Colorado not just with talent, but with arrogance and a downright offensive demeanor. Colorado had become a cakewalk for Oklahoma. The Sooners had won thirteen of our previous fourteen games and had averaged more than forty points a game in doing it. Colorado was one of the big reasons Oklahoma was turning out all-Americans and Heisman Trophy winners!

On the Thursday night before the 1987 game, I laid this on the team:

"No one is getting on that plane for the trip to Norman until he has looked me in the eye and told me, one on one, what I can expect of him."

Friday morning I set aside three hours and met, individually, in my office with the sixty Colorado football players who would be making the trip. Sixty men. Three minutes each. That's all it took. You see, there is tremendous power in the spoken word. When a man gives you his word, if he's worth his salt, he'll deliver on all that he promises.

When I summoned a player to my office and had him sit down across from me and look me in the eyes, I'd say, "Now, son, I want to know what I can expect from you when we go to Norman to play Oklahoma."

To a man, they'd look me squarely and say, "Coach, you can depend on me to bring it on every play. You can depend on me to play every down to the best of my ability. I'll play my best game ever against Oklahoma."

I'd tell each man I was holding him to his word, adding, "I want you to be positive, and excited so that all your teammates pick up on your attitude."

The sixty young men who boarded that plane were on a mission. Collectively, they would spend themselves in a valiant effort. I didn't know if there was any way we could win, but when I got on that airplane I knew we'd play the lights out. And we did.

It was a night game and nationally televised on ESPN, so I realized that a lot of the young men we were trying to recruit around the country would be watching. And before the night was over, they saw that we no longer would play dead dog! We indeed spent ourselves, trailed by just four points at halftime, and lost the game 24-6. The good news is that each of us knew we had given of ourselves for the team, that we had done the absolute best that we could do.

Still, it was no time to say, "Well, you can't ask for any more than that."

Because you can. You can ask more good players to come to school at Colorado because you've just proven that you have a solid foundation and that you are competitive. You can ask for more community support. You can ask for bigger crowds at home games. But mainly, you must ask for more of yourself.

We got to one level by having coaches who were judges in the front office. Then you have the media right on top of you, and these days, that relationship is adversarial most of the time.

No one understands how difficult it is to be a coach in these times. That's why I've always had such tremendous respect for Chuch Noll (of the Pittsburgh Steelers). I worked for him for eleven years, and the quality he has that sticks out more than any other single trait is consistency. Football is a game of peaks and valleys, but Noll is always the same. He doesn't get too pumped up during peak times, and doesn't get down when he's in the valleys. And that consistency carries through to the team. Noll has character and integrity.

McCartney has all those same ingrediants, and only a man like that could have weathered the kinds of storms he and his family have endured.

willing to work harder and longer hours, and be more diligent over a protracted period of time, which, in turn, has given us better players and more of them. And that has put us in a position where we can compete.

One of the first things that hit home with me when I first started reading God's word was the parable of the talents. We cannot, must not get all full of ourselves because of the brief success we've enjoyed. There's another level still to go, and you attain it only by proving that you belong, by being as good as the best year after year after year.

Consistency is, after all, the hallmark of true greatness.

Thirteen

The Recruiting War

B ennie Oosterbaan, a great player in his day and a highly successful coach at Michigan for some years starting in the late forties, once stood, arms folded, on the sidelines watching his team practice and told a writer standing next to him: "You want to know something? This recruiting business is going to drive me out of coaching."

Not long after that, Oosterbaan stepped aside to enjoy the rest of his life. He felt, as most coaches do, that recruiting had become a necessary evil.

It doesn't have to be evil, though it sometimes is—but it *is* necessary.

The simple matter of coaching football is just that—simple. It involves devising good plays (and let's face it, most play books are pretty much the same except for terminology). It involves devising a game plan you believe will work against a particular opponent. It involves the wise use of personnel. And it involves trying to motivate and inspire young men.

Simple? Sure. But unless you have beaten the bushes, traveled hundreds of thousands of miles, waited in a dingy office in a high school building in the hope you can catch a star player between classes, wangled a meeting with reluctant parents so you can tell them the advantages their son would have at your school, sparked an interest in both the young man and his folks, prayed that this quality athlete was also a quality student with good enough grades to gain admittance to your school—unless you've done all these things, you cannot begin to understand the complexities and ramifications involved in coaching.

I recruited when I was a high school coach and dealt with junior high boys, trying to persuade their parents to enroll them in Divine Child High School. I had something to sell—a good educational system and the chance to play for a school with a tradition of winning.

Nothing changed when I joined Bo Schembechler's staff at Michigan, except I was traveling more miles, working longer hours and dealing with high school seniors. I know in my heart I'm an excellent recruiter. I believe in what I'm doing and in the program I represent. I'm enthusiastic and I'm prepared. I try to make a whole-hearted presentation.

But when I came to Colorado, the program was in shambles. The dropout rate was terrible. So was the graduation rate. Fans were discouraged. The media was sick of the mediocrity. And a whole new perspective came into my recruiting efforts. Suddenly, here's what I had to sell: Colorado is a beautiful setting. The state, the community, the university, all beautiful. Yes, there's the reputation of being a "party school," but that's not so bad. There are lots of parties there. Lots of things to do. Lots going on. A fun place to play football and go to school.

I sold those things: a fresh start, a revitalization. And I told these youngsters they could be a factor in turning the program around; in bringing it to another level.

Sure, sometimes you feel like one of those cultists or a brush salesman, and sometimes you get doors slammed in your face. But you have to keep at it. All I ever try to do is give the facts and explain logic to each young man. In the early going, many of the young men I tried to recruit took one look at our program and assumed they should get to play right away. And most of the time, I'd have to tell them they couldn't do that.

Once in a great while, I find a talent—and everyone else has found it, too—that is so awesome you know it can be of immediate help. Such was the case not long ago with a young man named Ed King of Phenix City, Alabama. We were in a recruiting struggle and, as I remember, it boiled down to Colorado, Auburn and Alabama and at one stage he told me he thought he'd attend Colorado.

"If you do," I promised him, "you'll line up at guard

Bill McCartney

It didn't surprise a single coach when Jerry Claiborne suddenly announced after the 1989 season that he was resigning as football coach at Kentucky.

Here is a fine man, an outstanding coach who stood tall against the backdrop of the basketball scandal at this university. He recruited quality kids and won more games than most coaches would have under those circumstances, and he had a terrific mark for graduating his players.

He simply got worn out recruiting.

the first time you play as a freshman."

We didn't get him. He went to Auburn and made all-American as a sophomore.

In my early years, we weren't even in the ball park for that kind of talent. Try putting up seven victories in your first three seasons and then racing around the country trying to persuade top athletes to cast their lot with you. Hardly anyone wants a seat on the Titanic! I remember going into homes and knowing I had no chance. Sometimes the kid wouldn't even look me in the eye. He was seeing a loser and he didn't want any part of it.

When we began the 1986 season with those four losses, things got tough again. Try getting on an airplane after that and convincing a young man your program is really coming along and that if he'll just come to Colorado, he can make a difference.

I had to make a total change in my attitude in order to make any impact on these young men. I had to quit thinking like a loser—and begin counting my blessings—before I could really sell myself and my program to the young people of America.

> **Why couldn't every blue-chip athlete understand that by coming to Colorado, he'd be able to tell his children and his grand-children how, through the efforts of him and a select group of young men, they had rescued, restored and revitalized Buffalo football fortunes? That made perfect sense to me!**
> *Bill McCartney*

From that day on, when I found a recruit who put his head in his hands—who wouldn't look me straight in the eye—I determined that the problem was his, not mine. That was when I decided not to let him drag me down. And I went on to the next recruit. There are enough good people out there, you just have to find them and keep moving until you get enough guys who will listen to you.

When you've had a tough recruiting trip and gone from daylight until the late news and abused your stomach in fast-food places and are running on less than three hours sleep, you have two choices. You can get in your car after your last home visit and say to yourself that recruiting is evil, demeaning, unrewarding, unrelenting and that you're sick and tired of it all.

Or, you can remember the times when you put on a hard-hat and worked that construction job over the summer. You can think back to the poverty-stricken homes you have visited where seven or eight children are jammed into a house that is little more than a shanty, where you know there has rarely been enough to eat, where the clothes are patched-together rags and where equal opportunity is something politicians talk about and never a fact of life.

I choose number two. I think of how fortunate I am. I say to myself, God, I'm

Bo Schembechler:

Recruiting is ringing doorbells and selling. You go where the action is, you stay there and you work at it. There aren't any short cuts.

Bill McCartney never left anything undone; he was a dynamic recruiter. He knew what was important, he went in prepared and he sold Michigan football.

At Michigan, we always believed in positive recruiting. A lot of schools send guys in who tell a kid he'll get buried at Michigan, or maybe the kid is a C student and they try to steer him away from Michigan's high academic standards. They tell that student, "Come to our place. There's no such thing as ineligibility and you can still get an education."

Well, if a kid buys that crap, I didn't want him anyway. And if a kid didn't believe in his heart he could play for us, I didn't want him either.

lucky. I have a good job. I make good money. I'm doing what I love. I'm blessed with a marvelous wife who has, in truth, given up her whole life for me. I have four wonderful children and a beautiful grandchild. I am loved. I am appreciated. And on top of all that, I get to go into these peoples' homes and offer them something really worthwhile: I get to offer them what amounts to fifty-thousand dollars. I get to offer them the opportunity to attend one of the great universities in the country, to get an education, a chance to play football before big crowds and big television audiences, and to use all that as a stepping stone to a rich and rewarding life.

Just because not everyone accepts that offer should never make me think I have a tough job, or that I have failed.

The terrible downside to it all is what it takes away from family. We coaches are away from home so very much that our wives bear the task of raising the children.

When I *have* been home, we've tried to do things as a family. We've read Scripture together and prayed together. When we set aside special time in the summer for family things, we've often gone to Fellowship of Christian Athletes' gatherings where not only family ties, but spiritual ties are strengthened. When I've been on the road, Lyndi has often put affectionate notes in my suitcase— and over the years, there hasn't been more than a handful of nights I've missed calling home.

Still, sometimes you wake up wanting to put your arms around your wife and children and give them a hug—until you remember you're in a hotel on a roadside in Texas or California. I need to sit down more often with my children and explain to them that I have no excuses, no alibis for why I'm not home any more than I am. It's a choice I have made and while it requires much of me, it requires much more of my wife and our four children.

Lyndi McCartney:

In a way, being a coach's child is a dream: associating with the athletes, going to so many sporting events, being around the gym and the playing field.

But it's a nightmare as well. Our children just didn't spend the time with Bill they'd have liked. Bill never saw the boys play football until they were in high school. He saw very few of their basketball games through the years.

I used to plead with the Lord to give Bill time to watch his children play any kind of ball. Finally, the Lord answered my prayer and after spending a few afternoons with Bill, watching the boys play baseball and listening to Bill get on the umpires and unmercifully criticizing their calls, I said "uncle" to the Lord. "Take him back to work, Lord," I pleaded. "Why'd you ever listen to me in the first place?"

And the kids took a lot of grief over the years about their father's coaching. People somehow feel quite free to give the kids their opinions about Bill's coaching. You just have to learn to live with it, but it's a tough lesson not easily learned.

Bill's relationship with each child is terrific. Of course, there have been hurts and disappointments and struggles, but there is a very strong bond of love between him and each child.

It was odd, when a group had a roast for Bill last March in Denver, each of the kids had the opportunity to really zing the old man, and he would have understood that it was all

(Continued)

done in the spirit of fun. Even though some good-natured ribbing and some criticism is okay, and even expected, on those occasions, I doubt it ever occurred to my kids to take him to task.

Marc, a seventeen-year-old high school junior at the time, said: "You've really impressed and encouraged me as well as my friends, for always standing up for what you believe in. I love you, Dad."

Kristy, twenty-one, said: "You are the strongest and most loving person I know. I thank God you are my father and I feel like the luckiest daughter in the world. Thank you for loving me. I love you more than words can say."

Tom, our twenty-four-year-old teacher and coach, said: "Bill McCartney has been my coach, teacher, advisor, disciplinarian and best of all, my father. He has had a major impact on my life. His desire to see me grow as a teacher, coach and a spiritual man has influenced my life greatly. My father's spiritual maturity and his everlasting love for his family make me feel privileged and blessed to be his son. I love you, Dad."

Our twenty-five-year-old, Mike, added, "My dad means so much to me. He has been a leader in every facet of my life. Sometimes at work I get teased because I am exactly like my father in everything I do. The people I work with think it's funny how much I am like him. I receive this as the ultimate compliment. If I have the same characteristics as my parents, then I'll develop successfully in what's important in life. I am very lucky and blessed to have him as my father. I thank God every day."

(Continued)

While recruiting is tough on coaches and their families, there's certainly a downside for the athletes as well.

Sometimes word will spread like wildfire that some young man has that sure-fire, can't-miss tag, and recruiters will descend on him. Many of them may not have seen him play and may not have even seen film or tape on him—but they will have heard so many glowing reports that they'll try to talk him into picking their school as one of the five schools he's allowed to visit according to NCAA guidelines.

Maybe that young man has picked one school, and maybe he's begun telling the other schools that he's no longer interested in them.

Suddenly, the coaching staff at the favored school gets into a meeting and one assistant says, "You know, I was looking at this other prospect, and this kid we're pursuing couldn't handle him at all." That simple, disparaging word will chill their resolve to recruit the young man they thought was so good.

The other schools that were so hotly chasing this young player have already pulled out, and suddenly the kid is left to scramble late in the recruiting game to find another school that might be interested in him.

I watched this happen during our intensive recruiting right after the 1990 Orange Bowl. We were recruiting a young man in Texas and he made it clear right away he had no intention of going to Colorado. He'd already picked a school in the Southwest Conference. So I began to recruit one of his teammates, and when I went there for a visit, I learned of a terrible dilemma. As it turned out, the young man we had originally wanted had rejected opportunities to visit any other school save the one he had picked. Everyone else gave up on him because he was so firm in his decision to attend this particular school. Doggoned if he didn't get a telephone call from that school.

"Sorry," said the coach who'd been so aggressive just days before, "we're filled up at your position. We simply don't have a scholarship for you."

His high school coach made it clear that that school would no longer be welcome on his campus. And you can bet that this high school coach will make it extremely difficult for that school to recruit in his area again. He'll tell every one of his players how one of his star players was victimized.

And you know what? That kid was scrambling around to find someone who'd take him—and he's a sure-fire prospect, very capable of playing good football in a top-ranked program.

I do not lie to recruits. I tell them up front that we want them, but that we have only so many scholarships to offer. We may be looking to sign two quarterbacks, six running backs, four receivers, three linebackers, five linemen, five defensive backs and one kicker. But in order to get them, I'm probably talking with three, maybe four times that many players at each position. Since no one but Notre Dame can hand-pick, it generally boils down to a first-signed proposition. Inevitably, there are young men you would have taken as a matter of priority, had they reached a decision earlier in the recruiting process.

When you finally get these talented young men on campus, they have to make a big adjustment. They're with strangers, they're away from home for the first time, they're thrown in with people from different backgrounds and different cultures and frequently different sectors of the country. And, they're no longer the star of the team, but one of many players. And most of the time they're overwhelmed. Homesickness is a major problem, and if parents make the mistake of giving a kid a telephone credit card, believe me, he'll wear it out in the first year!

Parents may have done everything right in their home. They may have loved, supported, nurtured and prepared their son the best way they know how—but when that young person leaves home, his character is still in the balance. There are pressures and temptations and challenges that are brand new to him—and he is away from home and out from under the umbrella of protection and discipline. He no longer has to worry about the wrath of his folks should he have beer on his breath or marijuana or worse in his system.

It's been my experience that the young men who come from the good homes, the bedrock solid homes that are full of Christian love and care, are the ones who have the best chance to withstand all the pressures and to meet the academic and social challenges of life away from home.

The atmosphere on campus makes a big difference, too. I believe that a decent and caring coach has to provide an extended care facility away from home. I've heard some coaches say, "They're old enough to know right from wrong, they come here and they're pretty much on their own. I can't be account-able for all of them. I can't be everywhere, you know. I can't baby-sit ninety-five players."

Well, I believe you must do exactly that. You have to be responsible, and you are accountable if you have persuaded a young man to at-

When it came my turn, I merely said, "You are the only living person who can bring thunder and lightening, rainbows and sunshine, into my life on the same day. You are my man for all seasons and the love of my life and I thank God for you."

tend your school. Every player is a reflection on your leadership and on your school, and if they commit an indiscretion, it reflects on them, their family, their high school, their community.

Parents should look for the obvious indicators in the schools their sons are considering. For example, what is that coach's reputation for graduating his players? What is that coach's reputation for dealing with young people on an individual basis, for corralling them and helping them down the straight and narrow? What is that coach's reputation for fairness and decency, and what is that coach like as a husband and father?

Coaches go on the recruiting trail armed with statistics and graphic descriptions of the school. But you know what? The best recruiters in the world are your own players. If an athlete is having a positive experience, he'll communicate that to the recruits who visit your campus. If a high school senior comes to Colorado and sees young men who are sharp, who have class, who say and do the right things—then that's what counts. What your players are really saying to these potential teammates is, "Hey, this is a great place—we're on our way, we're catching fire here and why don't you come and join us?"

After our unprecedented 1989 season, I gave our recruiting co-ordinator, Rick George, a strong message to deliver to our present squad and to the recruits: *We're on our way. We're very, very close to being one of the best programs in all of college football. Now, the key is for us, can we recruit a great class?*

The first step toward winning is a huge one—recruiting good athletes with good character and good study habits and a willingness to suppress their own personal ambitions for the good of the team.

I couldn't have been more proud of our young people than I was during the 1989 season. Any negative things that had characterized our team in the past, well, that cloud had moved past us. In 1989, we were in the forefront all year with all the things going on both on and off the field, and our young people deported themselves beautifully. They won the attention of the nation with their performances on the field, and they won peoples' respect with their attitude and deportment off the field. They handled all that attention with dignity and humility and class. That's what happens when really good kids come together and believe in each other.

The difference in our program now, and way back when, is not only in the talent of the athletes, but in the caring, sharing attitude that's developed within the squad. We simply don't have room, and we won't make room, for selfish players.

Recruiting may be the part of college coaching the fan understands least. It's not a matter of simply sending out letters, looking at film and video tape someone sends to your office, then culling the crop to get the can't-miss talent. Recruiting is a twelve-month-a-year activity that gets frantic during the regular football season and impossible once the sea-

Joe Schmidt, all-pro line back for the Detroit Lions from 1953-65, member of the Pro Football Hall of Fame and head coach of the Lions 1967-72, is now a successful Detroit-area businessman. Said Schmidt:

I'm not an intimate, nor a confidant, but Bill strikes me as being a guy who lives his sermon instead of preaching it.

I had the opportunity to spend three days with him during the 1989 season and was on the sidelines for one of his big games. He lives and dies for his players. He's in tune with everything around him. The players respond to him. He takes time with every player, every problem. And he delegates responsibility well. Best of all, he doesn't have a huge ego. (You realize, of course, that coaches get big egos, too.)

son is over. I haven't kept track of the miles I've traveled in my career, but I probably have accumulated enough frequent flyer miles to accompany the Challenger space shuttle for a dozen orbits.

When I was on Bo Schembechler's staff at Michigan, I was responsible for recruiting the Detroit area. Since I grew up there and coached there, it was a natural for me. But after the national deadline had passed for signing letters of intent, I'd scour other parts of the country. I'd go to Florida with an accounting of all the players signed by Southeastern Conference schools and other schools with top programs. These were the top high school seniors in the area. They'd been heavily recruited and courted by many top schools and now the pressure was off. And some of them felt abandoned once all the excitement wore off.

I'd seek them out, see if they had used up their allotted campus visits, and if not, I'd encourage them to pay us a visit and look around, since signing with a Southern school wasn't binding if a young man chose to come to a Big Ten school instead.

In the late seventies, we went after a lanky receiver I'll call Terry Jones. He was from a high school in Pompano, Florida, and Terry had been first team all state in football and third team all state in basketball, so we're talking about an outstanding athlete here. And he was a fine young man, to boot. Terry had already signed with a school in the South, but he agreed to visit Michigan—perfectly legal and on the up-and-up since Michigan is a Big Ten school.

The weekend Terry visited, we got hit with a tremendous snowstorm. I reckon it was the first time Terry had every seen snow and he and this other recruit went out on a couple of snowmobiles and raced around the University of Michigan golf course. The one recruit came back after a reasonable amount of time, but no Terry. I was about to form a search party when he pulled in, a smile as big as Texas on his face.

I don't think he quit grinning the entire weekend. He had a

great time, and when it was over he just said, "Coach, this is the place for me."

But as we drew near the signing deadline, Terry informed me that his parents wouldn't sign the letter of intent for him to attend Michigan. I told him we'd work through the problem once I got to Florida on deadline day.

When I arrived in Pompano, Terry's first words to me were, "Coach, it's not even close. They're not about to let me come to Michigan. They won't even consider it."

I stayed in Pompano for days, waiting for a break. It's a helpless feeling that every coach has experienced a dozen times or more.

Terry's high school coach struck me as a decent and fair man who wanted the best for Terry. He realized, as I did, that Michigan was Terry's choice. My next move was to ask the coach to intervene with the parents, to tell them that if they forced the kid to go somewhere against his will, it

Bill McCartney:

After the 1989 season, the turnaround in our fortunes on the field had created a brand new atmosphere! The coaches we sent on the recruiting trail were much more enthusiastic, and recruits across the nation far more receptive.

The good ones always want to play in big games before big television audiences— and the Colorado Buffs were about to play for the national championship against the legendary Fighting Irish of Notre Dame.

could be something he would regret, and might hold against them for a long time.

Next day, the coach called me and told me he thought it was all worked out, but that it'd be necessary for Coach Schembechler to fly in to finalize the deal. The parents would feel better, he thought, talking to the main man.

I couldn't conceal my excitement when I got Bo on the phone. It was a major coup for us and Bo agreed to get the next plane for Fort Lauderdale—but only after he asked, "Are you sure I have to fly down there?" I told him it was essential for wrapping up matters.

Bo couldn't have been any further south than Toledo when the high school coach called me again.

"Don't bring him in," he warned, "we have a roadblock here."

The roadblock was that the other school had offered to buy a brand new station wagon for the parents once they delivered their son.

There was no question about a great need in the home. It was small, rundown and full of children. A new car must have been an irresistible temptation for people living in such poverty.

I had a talented young man who wanted to come to Michigan, parents who had yielded to the temptation of illegal recruiting and done what they thought was best for them, a high school coach who was caught in the middle, and a boss who'd be frothing at the mouth when he learned he'd made a trip in vain.

I told the coach I'd expect him at the home when Bo got there for his visit, and he agreed. I made it clear that Michigan wouldn't be a part of any gift-giving.

The minute we walked into that little house, the kid gave Bo a big smile. They hit it off right away and there wasn't any doubt where Terry wanted to go. We sat down and Bo said to the mother:

"Mrs. Jones, your son has strongly indicated he wants to attend the University of Michigan. You have my promise that we'll do everything we can to see that he gets a good education, and he'll get every opportunity to play. It's just what a mother would want for her son."

She didn't say one word. Instead she turned—even adjusted her chair—so she wouldn't have to face Bo. He kept his poise, though it was clear she would do no talking that day. Not to us anyway.

"Mrs. Jones," Bo said, "if you won't talk to us, maybe we'd better talk to your husband."

"My husband's working," she shot back, without giving him a glance.

Mr. Jones was working as some sort of security guard at a place where they were cutting out a new development deep in the woods. I'd rented a sub-compact car in order to save the school money—and had stayed free with my parents, who were at that time living in Pompano—and we all piled into that little car. There was myself, Bo, the high school coach and Terry, who was all of six-feet-five. He said he thought he knew where his dad was working.

It was getting along into the early evening hours and we plunged deeper and deeper into the Everglades, looking for Terry's father. It seems like we wandered around for hours. Bo was getting more upset by the minute. We had reservations on a mid-evening plane and he kept glancing at his watch.

Finally, we were surrounded by swampland, it was dusk, hard to see, and Bo ran out of patience.

"Let's go," he snapped, probably figuring that since he had built a tradition of victories based on running games instead of passing games, what did he really need with a wide receiver anyway?

Just then, Terry spotted some heavy equipment—the stuff his dad was supposed to be guarding as the workmen turned this swampland into viable real estate.

"I think that's my dad's car," he announced, as he peered down this forbidding lane that had been cut out of the morass.

In we went, and sure enough, there sat the Jones' vehicle—but no Mr. Jones as far as we could see. Terry had cautioned us that his dad carried a gun as part of his job. We beamed our lights right on the car, head to head.

Suddenly, as if turned loose by a coil spring, this body reared up in the front seat. Then the figure—which apparently had been sleeping—disappeared.

I can't speak for the others in the party, but I was scared out of my head. Terry volunteered to check things out and I didn't argue with him. After a moment, he waved to us that it was all right for the rest of us to get out.

When we got to the car, it was clear that Mr. Jones had been over-served. A little too much of the grape had required him to take a siesta.

We stepped out of the car and into nothing but goo. Bo had on a dandy-looking suit and he was wearing a pair of those expensive alligator loafers. He hiked up his pants and tried to step gingerly, but it was a losing battle and Bo wasn't liking it one bit. When he went face-to-face with the man in the car, Bo got right to the point:

"Mr. Jones, I'm Bo Schembechler from Michigan. I'm here to sign up your son Terry. He wants to come to Michigan."

The man was barely audible. He mumbled, "Okay."

"We're gonna sign these papers right here, Mr. Jones," Bo commanded.

Then Bo had one order for the young man.

"Come over here, Terry, and bend over so we can sign this thing."

And doggoned if Bo didn't put the paper on Terry's back, and in the lights of the car in that swamp, Bo signed for Michigan and Mr. Jones scribbled his name on the letter of intent. Terry's coach witnessed the whole thing as it unraveled. Bo quickly thanked Mr. Jones and the four of us piled back into that washtub of a car and sped away.

The flight we were to be on was the last thing smokin' to

Detroit and we made good time until we got to the Fort Lauderdale Airport, where we faced what appeared to be a mile-long line of stopped traffic. Schembechler had one last order left in him that night:

"Bill, get in the other lane. We're gonna miss the flight."

"But Coach, this is a two-lane road, and that lane's for oncoming traffic."

"Never mind, just do it."

You do some crazy things as an assistant coach, but this would be one for the records. I swerved into the other lane and punched the pedal. As soon as we saw the first sign that said Delta Airlines, Bo bolted out of the car and left me sitting there. The coach volunteered to return the rental car for us, and I caught up with Bo as we sped through that terminal like a pair of O.J. Simpsons.

Bo and I have been close for a lot of years and I've never seen him drink all that much, but this happened to be one of those champagne flights. That night, the coach of the Michigan Wolverines did a pretty good job on a bottle of the bubbly all by himself.

Hollywood—California, not Florida—could write a fantastic ending to this story, telling how Terry came to Michigan and won a place on the team and in the hearts of the fans, becoming a star of such epic proportions that his name would be forever remembered whenever people spoke in revered tones about University of Michigan football.

But the true story is that Terry Jones never caught a pass in a football game at Michigan. His career was marred by an assortment of injuries, including a broken finger as our team was preparing for the 1979 Rose Bowl. But he did something he wanted to do. . .

. . . he attended the University of Michigan . . . and he did something else for which the university's football program will always be grateful.

Terry Jones was very influencial in Michigan's efforts to successfully recruit Anthony Carter, the celebrated pass catcher who broke every Michigan receiving record. As things turned out, no Michigan fan could ever forget A.C. Terry Jones never even got a football letter at Michigan, but in all fairness he should get an award of merit for talking Carter into coming north.

Fourteen

A.C.

The late Woody Hayes was credited with saying it. Woody claimed he first heard it from Darrell Royal when Coach Royal was at Texas. But Bo Schembechler believed it:

"There are three things that can happen when you pass the football, and two of them are bad."

In an interview only weeks before he died, Coach Hayes amended it, saying that another bad thing can happen: you can get fired. He was referring to the Gator Bowl incident in which a Clemson player intercepted an Ohio State pass late in the game. Coach Hayes let his frustration get away from him and he threw a punch at the Clemson player. Days later, then-athletic director at Ohio State, Hugh Hindman, fired Hayes. It was the end of a long and distinguished career with the Buckeyes.

Bo Schembechler loved Woody Hayes. He didn't always agree with everything his old coach said or did, but friends don't have to agree all the time. Being a disciple, Bo had no love affair with the forward pass. The way you win, Bo believed, was the way Woody won, the way Patton won—on the ground, with tough troops willing to grind it out yard by yard. In football, you win first of all by having the ball more than your opponent has it. You accomplish that with a strong defense, a good kicking game, advantageous field position and a methodical ground game. In his early seasons, Bo endured a lot of criticism even when he won.

Given a choice, Schembechler would take a gritty quarterback who was durable if not fast, tough if not sleek. Bo liked quarterbacks who could make good decisions, run with the football when asked to, and pass it when absolutely necessary.

It is axiomatic that high school recruits are automatically attracted to programs suited to their specific talents. Thus, it was one of the great recruiting coups of all time when we persuaded Anthony Carter to play football at Michigan.

Anthony had staggering high school statistics, scoring fifty-nine touchdowns, an all-American in both football and basketball. He's still the fastest person I've ever seen on a football field, and he had so much speed in basketball that he'd get the ball at the end of the court on an in-bounds pass, and still beat everybody else down the floor on the fast break. He was playing basketball when I first saw him and talked him into coming to Michigan as one of his five on-campus visits.

That, in itself, was a major accomplishment, since he never seemed more than lukewarm about the whole thing. I'm sure he wouldn't even have agreed to a visit had not some of his close advisers spoken so highly about the school and about Bo Schembechler. Besides, Anthony had already signed a letter of intent with Florida State, and that discouraged a lot of schools. But in those years, that signing wasn't binding on Big Ten schools, and we pulled out all the stops to ensure an impressive visit to the Michigan campus.

Everything cooperated except the weatherman.

It never got above zero the entire weekend! Knowing that

Anthony was accustomed to the Florida sunshine, we decided to be as resourceful as possible. We got a special permit from the Wayne County Sheriff's Department at Metropolitan Airport outside Detroit and parked a jeep close to the spot where Anthony would exit the airport. And whoosh! Right off the plane, right into a vehicle that had been left running with the heater turned up *very* high. All weekend long, we did things door-to-door whenever possible, and when we did have to step outside with him, we jumped into one heated vehicle after another.

Not once during the entire weekend did I get any indication that Carter was giving Michigan a second thought. He was being accommodating, that's all. I took the plane back to Florida with him since I had to go there for additional recruiting, and I kept the conversation going by reminding him of all the advantages that would be his by joining the Wolverines.

"There's one thing you'll have to overcome if you decide to sign with Michigan," I told him. "You'll have to face the fact we do have some winter here."

He turned and looked straight at me and said, "You know, it's not all that cold there."

I knew then our plan had worked, but we didn't seem all that much closer to getting Anthony Carter. In fact, I realized we were a distant third behind Florida State and Texas. But when the national signing day arrived, Carter didn't sign with anyone.

I arrived in town late Wednesday afternoon. I tried to get an appointment to see Anthony on Thursday but was unsuccessful. Friday afternoon I happened across Carter on the street. I was driving a rental car, he was riding a bicycle. I pulled up alongside and asked if I could talk to him. He just stared at me and pedaled away.

His basketball team was starting state tournament play that night and won the game, meaning another game the following night. I stayed around, knowing I was playing a long shot. Carter's team was beaten the second night, a Saturday. I stuck around through Sunday, and still hadn't even had a chance to make a final appeal.

Monday morning dawned. I wolfed down some breakfast and headed for Suncoast High School, trying one last time to see Anthony. I saw his coach instead.

"I've been here since last Wednesday, Coach," I pleaded, "and all I want is five minutes with Anthony. If he tells me *no*, or absolutely won't talk to me, then I'm on the next plane to Michigan. But I want to hear it from him."

The coach agreed to get Anthony between classes. In five minutes he returned, telling me Carter hadn't come to school that morning. The coach had called Anthony at home, encouraging him to give me just five minutes. While Carter had agreed, the coach alerted me that Anthony might not be in the best of moods. Apparently he'd been up all night. Anthony's girlfriend, who was going to college in another part of the state, had managed to get into town and Anthony, the girl and a recruiter from another school had spent the night in the recruiter's car, talking.

But there was a part to the story that neither the coach nor I had discovered yet: It seems that Anthony's mother had gotten up in the early dawn to get ready to go to her job as a cleaning lady in a small motel in town. She found the threesome, still together after a night spent in the recuiter's car. It was then Anthony told her he had made his decision about college. And it wasn't Michigan.

Mrs. Carter, a tiny woman, looked up at that recruiter and told him, "You take that girl and dangle her in front of my son like that? I'll never sign for my son to go to your school."

Mrs. Carter was gone by the time I arrived and knocked at the door. Anthony came to the door, glanced at me for a second and, without saying a word, sort of shoved the screen door open. Then he walked away. It was clear to me what he was saying: Come in if you must, say what you have to, and then leave.

I'd had six days to get my spiel down and I wasn't going to blow it then. I pulled up a chair and sat facing him.

"Anthony, I've been here six days now and all I want is a

chance to talk with you. I'm going to take just ten minutes and after that, if you don't like what I've said, you'll never see me again."

I did every bit of the talking. I never asked one question. I just told him what Michigan had to offer—no special inducements, no prizes, no deals, just a chance to get a great education and play in a great program. And I told him everyone else had probably told him that Bo Schembechler was a running coach and that he'd be wasting his talents there. Bo's stubborn and Bo's a bear on defense and strong running and good kicking—but Bo's also a true pro. I assured Carter his talents would be utilized.

When I finished, I merely said, "That's it. What do you think?"

Anthony Carter, in cold, simple terms, looked at me and asked, "Where do I sign?"

I almost fell off the chair.

He said we'd have to go to the motel to see his mom. When we arrived there, Anthony told her, "This is the coach from Michigan. I'm going to Michigan. We need you to sign papers."

She signed them but Anthony didn't. He said he wanted to go to school so his coach could witness the signing. Once at school, doggoned if we could find the head coach. I was frantic, thinking Anthony might change his mind before we could complete the transaction. After all, just a couple of hours earlier he'd been all set to go somewhere else. We finally located an assistant coach, and Anthony agreed to sign in his presence. Once his name was on the paper, I telephoned Schembechler. He was flabbergasted. He chatted with Anthony briefly, and then I told Bo he just had to come to Florida for the formal announcement. Bo was on the first plane leaving Detroit Metro.

You want a storybook ending to this? The first time Anthony Carter touched the ball as a freshman, he ran seventy-six yards for a touchdown with a punt return. He scored thirty-seven touchdowns for the Wolverines, averaging a gain of 17.4 yards every time he came in contact with the football at Michigan. He gained more yards per play than any person who ever played college football. He became a three-time all-American, was named captain of his team and got his degree before becoming a millionaire with his extraordinary exploits in the National Football League.

And to get him to come to Michigan, it took two things—lots of hard work and lots of luck. I just happened to be in the right place at the right time.

In the four years immediately preceding Carter's arrival at Ann Arbor, Michigan completed 273 passes in 593 attempts for 4,616 yards. A.C.—*After Carter*—the figures ballooned to 494 completions in 955 passes for 7,419 yards.

But great as he was—and his name will always be remembered not only by Michigan and Big Ten fans, but by anyone considering the truly remarkable athletes of all time—Carter learned to put his team first. He became dedicated and selfless, disciplined and industrious. And in the end, he was accorded the highest honor a Michigan player can achieve: he was selected team captain for his senior year.

Fifteen

The Coach's Role: Motivator, Manager and Defender

One of the ways that I believe I can touch young lives with a positive influence is by coaching football. I'm not suggesting it's a noble calling, but I honestly believe it's what God wants me to do right now.

In the more than twenty-five years I have been coaching, I have tried to instill in these young men a sense of responsibility and discipline and accountability as well. And as far as I'm concerned, any kind of discipline that strives to prepare young men for *life*, and not just for the scoreboard, has to include the development of their hearts and souls. To capture it in a phrase, I've tried to motivate our athletes on the field—and toward even larger pursuits off the field.

The American Civil Liberties Union can—and did—stop me from what it called "forcing my beliefs" on my players. But neither the ACLU nor any other group can keep me from sharing my beliefs with the world:

. . .I can't make my team engage in group prayer before or after a game, but I can do my best to live the kind of life that sets a good example for my players.

. . .I can't impose my will on my athletes and require them to attend our chapel service, but I can schedule such a service and make it available to anyone who wants to attend.

. . .And I can—and will—keep right on praying that every athlete who commits himself to playing football for Colorado will also commit his life to Jesus Christ. By precept and example, my goal is to show each player that Jesus was not a wimpy, indecisive person, but a strong and powerful person who drew men to Him; that He was an imposing and persuasive man of incomparable leadership.

Before the 1987 season, it was the feeling of our coaching staff that we had made significant progress in our program—but it still wasn't enough. We were recruiting strong, working hard, and now it was time to focus on motivation.

In July, just before our squad was to check in for late summer workouts, I wrote to each player, encouraging them to embrace responsibility; to strive to be leaders of championship caliber; and to motivate themselves toward excellence. I closed by saying, "If you want to have a great team, report in the greatest shape of your life."

The squad was better, but not good enough to get to the top of the heap. Our 7-4 record left us trailing the best teams in the Big Eight and bypassed for post-season bowl consideration.

The following year, in March, we set the theme for the 1988 season: "Dare to be great!" We had every right to think we could be as good as Oklahoma and Nebraska and I wanted to be certain our players understood that we would no longer be an automatic victory on the tough guys' schedules.

That summer, I wrote a letter to our entire squad, using Raymond Berry as an example of a player who achieved greatness not through God-given athletic skills, but through dedication. Berry was undersized, slow, one leg was shorter than the other; he had asthma, wore glasses—and still he's the man whose name is mentioned most frequently when pro-football fans talk about the greatest pass receivers in the history of the National Football League.

I asked the Colorado Buffs:

How about you? Do you have an added dimension to your resolve? Do you persevere when others draw back? Are you motivated to go above and beyond what might normally be expected? Encourage one another. Call your teammates frequently. Challenge one another. Rally the weak. Inspire the sleeper. Accept no excuses. This is your team. Demonstrate a powerful positive presence . . . . Colorado football is holding you accountable to be the very best you can be.

Two months later, I wrote our players a long letter and told them the story of Wilma Rudolph, who was born prematurely and had a host of childhood ailments including a terrible bout with polio that left her with a crooked left leg and a foot twisted inward. Wilma Rudolph endured metal braces, stares from neighborhood kids and six years of bus rides to Nashville for special therapy—and she became an Olympic champion. I wrote our players:

Proverbs 4:23 says, "Keep your heart with all diligence, for out of it spring the issues of life." There are endless examples of how ordinary athletes have achieved extraordinary results. Often we discover they were merely willing to pay the price to live out a dream.

I wanted our players to think big, to live out a dream.

How was I to know in midsummer of 1988—just weeks before Kristy would discover that she was pregnant by Sal Aunese and months before Sal would be diagnosed with inoperable cancer—that our dream would include a nightmare as well?

In July of that year I noted that our weight room was the busiest it had been in seven summers. Could it be that our message—all the reminders and all the motivational tips—were getting through? Yet it wasn't enough that we simply had more quality athletes, or that our athletes were taking more initiative.

We still needed to become a *team*.

On July 12 I wrote our players:

> A legitimate team member is loyal. This means he is committed to each player and coach twenty-four hours a day. He respects each guy regardless of class, culture, creed or color. He defends each man behind closed doors or in public view. He refuses to put down or slander his teammate under any circumstances. He allows for differences and always gives his teammate the benefit of the doubt. He offers an opinion about a teammate only when it presents a positive and supportive posture. If he has offended a teammate, he willingly goes to him and resolves the problem.

Only by coming together completely as a team could we generate the power to conquer.

On July 20 I again took a verse out of Proverbs for them. I reminded our athletes that "as a man thinketh in his heart, so is he." Many of our players—as well as players at every other college and university across the land—come from difficult and sometimes totally unacceptable home environments. But a successful man will achieve despite his circumstances, while the failure always blames his environment. I urged our players to prepare for success rather than readying their alibis.

As we stood on the threshold of the 1989 season—shortly after T.C. was born and in the face of Sal's illness—I sensed that the year offered Colorado the rare opportunity to reach the highest plateau in college football. We needed to find that extra something to get us through the tough games.

The old-time baseball manager, John McGraw, used to say that the way to success was to beat the daylights out of the weaker teams and to break even with the good ones. But baseball has a drawn-out season of games played between April and October and there's room for occasional slumps. Championship football teams cannot afford the luxury of a slump. A college football season is more like a World Series in baseball, except that to be the very best, you have to sweep the series.

In 1989, Colorado had enough good football players to win. But we needed an "attitude" to match our physical abilities.

For 1989, we adopted the slogan: "A quest for glory."

That June I told our players:

I was hired to coach CU on June 10, 1982. Saturday marks my seventh anniversary. Much has changed over these seven years. Every phase of our program has achieved enormous growth. Academically, we were selected by the College Football Association for special merit in graduating our players. Our current team was recently ranked eighth in the nation by *Sporting News* in their pre-season selections. In addition, you can take great pride in knowing that you are playing in a clean and honest program.

I tried to spur our players to accept the challenge, to commit to the quest for glory. I wanted them to have lofty ideals. I didn't think it was too much to ask of them.

A week later, I set down four points for the squad's consideration. I wrote:

In order to maximize our abilities we need to be fed four ways every day:

1) Physically. If your nutritional intake is proper, you have more energy. If your diet is sound you will build muscle. If you are exercising and working out faithfully, your cardiovascular fitness is enhanced.

2) Mentally. Read the newspapers—not just the sports pages. Be informed on a variety of issues. Take pride in being able to discuss national and local problems and situations. Listen to what informed people are saying.

3) Emotionally. We need support. We need friends. We need confidants. We need family. Develop these relationships. Demonstrate fierce loyalty and trust in your people. These commitments help sustain us when things are tough.

4) Spiritually. Most people try to cope with little or no spiritual food. At best, they attend church once a week and that's it. Their lives are often characterized by ups and downs, highs and lows, mountains and valleys. They really can't deal with the adversity or even good fortune that comes into their lives. Daily prayer and reading scripture are the things that root out sins in our lives.

I closed with these words: "Take pride in being a man of substance. Cultivate moderation and balance in your life. Be operating on all cylinders when you hit camp in August."

By the end of the 1989 season—our Golden Season—we had satisfied that quest for glory. We knew what it was like to be a team. We had tasted success. . . realized a dream.

But even in the face of successes like these, I know that my job as coach is only partly fulfilled. The young men I lead demand much more of me than that.

Vince Lombardi was once quoted as saying that football is not a democracy; rather, it is a dictatorship. If it is, I would hope it is a benevolent dictatorship. It is imperative that a coach listen to his players; that he communicate that he cares about them as individuals, that he attempt, at least, to understand the often difficult circumstances of their lives.

Most critical of all, I believe a coach needs to remember that these young men are being thrust into what I believe is a totally permissive society. Some psuedo-experts refer to it as the "new morality." What that really means is no morality at all.

I alluded to it earlier by saying that if the average mother and father had any idea of what goes on around college campus, they'd think twice—maybe three times—about sending their offspring to campus. It is not at all uncommon to see cocaine flaunted in dormitories, or for a student of one sex to come to another student's room, uninvited, crawl into bed and offer sexual favors.

Lyndi McCartney:

When young men come to Colorado to play football, our coaches and their families provide unconditional love for them. Yes, they get yelled at. Yes, they get criticized. They get corrected and reprimanded. They're not unlike a family, with everyone committed to everyone else.

Our lives are a shared experience for a few years Some of the players sense that connection; reach out and accept it, return it and cherish it always. Some never feel the spirit of love They get hung up in personal difficulites and in anger and resentment. They put up walls that love cannot penetrate.

But the love will be there for them, whenever they need it. If the Lord waited on me all these years, the least we can do as His children is to have a bountiful supply of love on hand if another of His children has a need.

It takes a young person of enormous character and willpower to resist such temptation. "Just say no" doesn't get the job done. No amount of counseling can adequately prepare a college fresh-man for the lifestyle that lies immediately ahead. As a coach or instruc-tor or counselor or advisor, you merely do what you can and hope for the best.

While I take great pains to deal with football issues, I'm not at all reluctant to deal with emotional and spiritual issues as well.

Morality is one of these issues. Another issue, quite frankly, that demands my attention is racism.

Bill Russell practically revolutionized professional basketball be-cause of the way he played defense, a model for all those who have performed since his days with the Boston Celtics. Russell is a former colleague of my co-author at ABC Sports, and he once explained the frustration he felt at the racial injustice inflicted on him and his family:

"For the most part," Russell explained, "Celtic fans loved me so long as I was out there in my green and white uniform doing my thing as an athlete. They cheered my every move. But they didn't feel the same way about me when I put on my street clothes and tried to buy a house in one of the better sections of Boston, so the Russell children could enjoy the benefits of a good environment and a good school system. That's when I became just another nigger."

Boulder, Colorado is a great community. The McCartney family loves it and its people and there is every reason in the world to believe that we could be comfortable in this environment for the remainder of our lives.

But it is not a perfect community—any more than the young athletes we bring into Boulder are perfect people—and some members of the community have been slow, or even unwilling, to try to understand the minority athlete.

At one time, we went through a two-year stretch where every

off-the-field altercation we experienced involved a black or Samoan athlete. Some of these incidents have been serious offenses and I'm not suggesting they were less than that; but many of them were not as serious as people were led to believe. Sometimes it seemed to me that the police and some members of the community over-reacted.

When we first started having incidents with our minority athletes in the community, I'm sure I was paranoid, perhaps blaming one side over the other. But I've come to see there are two sides to the problem. There are people in the community who see the black or minority athlete as an invasive force within the community, who view him as a threat, a menace, without ever knowing a thing about the athlete as an individual. You also have students on campus who have been raised in a predominantly white community, who may never have been in the company of minorities, and who may have been fed wrong information and bitterness from their parents or their community.

And sometimes you'll have a minority athlete who comes to an all-white community with his own fears and paranoia and, as a result, he may be waiting for the first provocation, the first sign that somebody may have a prejudice or bias of some kind. And he overreacts.

These dynamic together go a long way toward creating a volatile situation.

Today's college students—of every race—are young and are

> **The CU program is engaged in what I consider to be an extraordinary effort to ensure good behavior on the part of the players, as well as excellent community relations. But the limelight is on the athlete such that when something does occasionally happen, it is reported with more vigor than something that might occur with any other student.**
>
> *Hal Nees*
> *Division Chief of Patrol*
> *Boulder Police Dept.*

forming their characters and personalities. They need to think things through and see for themselves what the real world is all about. Give these young people time together, and chances are they'll experience a healing and come to understand that every man should be judged on his own merit, and not on the color of his skin.

A year or so ago, I got a wonderful telephone call from Pat Bowlen, who owns the Denver Broncos. He had read about some of our difficulties—in particular, the problems some of our black athletes were facing. All he wanted to know was this: "What can I do to help?" I asked him to send us a group of prominent black players who'd gone to predominantly white schools. I wanted these men to talk and interact with our players.

It happened, and from all reports I got, it was a great session. I didn't attend, because I didn't want to influence anything that was said. But it was good therapy for our players. They could ask tough questions and get straight answers. They could hear, first-hand, from black athletes who had made it in the pros, but who'd made it through some struggles off the field, as well; athletes who had surely endured some prejudice. The way I understand it, the Bronco players told our young guys about life in the real world— what they could do to better prepare themselves not just to survive, but to thrive and prosper in it.

In recent years, we've had a clinical psychologist, a black man named Dr. Will Miles, working closely with many of our students athletes, black and white, and it's done a tremendous amount of good. The result we see now more than ever is that when these young people can talk things through, deal openly with their own frustrations and angers and fears and doubts and misgivings and put all the misinformation out on the table, they're able to do the sound, rational thing and not respond in an impulsive, irrational manner that simply heightens the problem.

Dr. Harry Edwards has been a trailblazer in race relations within the sports community, and when he was on our campus in the spring of 1989 he pointed out that when you go through a town like Boulder, there are very few things, aesthetically, that reinforce to a black man or woman that he or she belongs here. We need more expressions of black culture around our community. I address these issues as I speak around the community. I want people to be aware of these needs. Many times, bad things happen not because someone is mean-spirited, but because that person simply is not enlightened.

I'm aware that not everyone shares my views. "Why doesn't he just coach the football team?" they ask. "Why doesn't he tend to the business of football instead of involving himself in the major social issues of our time?"

Because I'm not just a football coach, that's why! I'm a human being with a wife and four children, and my life isn't just all football. I'm concerned about the kind of society in which we live. I care about the educa-

Dave Evans, captain of the University of Colorado Police Department:

The eighteen- to twenty-two-year-old age group is the most trouble-prone in the country, and it doesn't matter whether they're college students or just young adults out of high school. I also think that the transient population in any college town creates less of a feeling of ownership toward the community and this, combined with the age factor, creates a real potential for problems.

But the problems we've had in Boulder, with the Colorado University student-athletes, aren't unique at all to athletes. The average football player at Colorado is basically no different than the average guy going to class, except he's bigger. I can't speculate why there was so much publicity here and nationally about

(Continued)

tional system we have designed for our children. I worry about the environment and I wonder whether we are slowly destroying ourselves and our world. It bothers me that a task force on racial tension reported recently that animosity and indifference by white students toward blacks at the University of Florida is a major problem that needs to be confronted.

Yes, indeed, I fret about the world today. But don't send me any anonymous letters telling me to mind my own business. This world *is* my business—just as it should be everyone's. Besides, I get all the vile anonymous mail I can handle, anyway. The hate-mail I get is rarely signed; there is never a return address. But the Lord has given me the strength and the wisdom to deal with things like that.

I've decided that I can't changed the world, but I can influence my little part of it—whether I'm dealing with community race issues, building interracial relationships among the athletes, or motivating a young man to reach for the stars in every area of his life.

Not long ago I saw a cartoon of a doctor who had just delivered a screaming baby to a mother, and he said, "I just deliver 'em, lady, I don't explain 'em." Well, I'm more than just a football coach—I deliver players to the university and then I have to explain them. No, I cannot account for all of their misadventures, but I can try to make them accountable. I can't explain the circumstances of their lives, but I can try to make them want to improve their chances and abilities, on and off the field.

I've seen tremendous improvement from our student-athletes of all colors and race! And still, we haven't done enough. I'd like to be able to put the term "gentleman-scholar-athlete" beside the name of every player we recruit. I want our players to be gentle as well as strong. I want them to be well-mannered as well as courageous. I want them to be confident yet humble.

In the ancient days when chariot racing was a big sport, they'd bring six great racing horses together and harness them so they'd run as a team. The implement used to harness the great beasts was called a "humility."

Colorado players, except that perhaps timing and the need for news at that moment had something to do with it.

I think it's important to note that we make a real effort to treat individuals as just that. Athletes are neither coddled nor are they singled out. And we've never been asked by any individual or group on campus to treat one group with any different kind of consideration.

There's a healthy dialogue between the police and the athletic department. We work very closely with individual coaches, and if we feel we have a concern about a player, we can talk with them. Conversely, if the coaches feel they have a concern about a stance an officer or our department has taken, they feel comfortable approaching us.

I'm a Buff fan and I've attended every football game that's been played in Folsom Stadium since 1970, and I'd have to say that the behavior of some fans can be far worse than the behavior of the players!

The whole situation here is comfortable, and much better than it was four, five or six years ago. But you have to realize, too, that when good things are happening, they don't get very much attention—if something not so good happens, there's a big splash in all the papers.

Humility is the harnessing of power—and humility, to my way of thinking, boils down to knowing who you are before God. It's a hard, hard lesson for young and talented athletes to learn they need something more than their God-given skills—that they need humility, too. King Saul of Israel was a tall man of majestic stature—yet power went to his head and ruined him. In Proverbs we're told about the things the Lord hates—a proud look, a lying tongue, hands that shed innocent blood, a heart that devises wicked imaginations, feet that are swift to mischief, a false witness that speaks lies and one who sows discord among brethren.

As I search the Bible, time after time I am struck by powerful messages on the necessity of humility.

Galatians 6:3 tells us: "For if anyone thinks himself to be something, when he is nothing, he deceives himself."

Ever since I gave my life to Jesus Christ in 1974, I have known that without Jesus in my life, Bill McCartney is nothing. I read in Romans 12:3: "For I say, through the grace given unto me, to everyone who is among you, not to think of himself more highly than he ought to think, but to think soberly, as God has dealt to each one a measure of faith."

I'm grateful for our successes and the honors that have accompanied our victories, however without God in my life, not only would the good things never have been possible, but the McCartney family would never have had the strength to endure the tribulations that came with our season of glory.

As long as I live, I'll remember the beautiful words Lyndi wrote in our Christmas greeting of 1989, not too long after Sal's death and T.C.'s birth. She told our loved ones:

"The walls of our home seemed to melt away this past year, being replaced with glass and laying our lives open for all eyes. Although there was great pain, there was also tremendous joy. Living in a glass house has its advantages—the 'Son' shines in every corner. Love, joy, peace, patience, kindness, goodness, faithfulness, gentleness and self-control—combined with forgiveness and an abundance of humility—truly describe our year."

She closed by telling everyone, "I'm overwhelmed by the grace of God in our lives."

Only a woman of God—a woman of great humility—could endure what she and our family faced and yet maintain that kind of outlook.

I recently came across a wondrous quote from the late William Temple, Archbishop of Canterbury. He said that humility is not thinking more of yourself than you ought to think; humility is not thinking less of yourself than you ought to think; humility is not thinking of yourself at all.

Now, *that* speaks to my heart.

Dr. Will Miles, clinical psychologist, is currently working with Colorado athletes:

Society has changed in the past ten, fifteen years—and the change is not all for the good. We were at a high at what we might call the Kennedy/Dr. King era. The 1964 Civil Rights Act opened the door for full participation, for massive integration on college campuses.

But today, society is more polarized and there is more racism than in previous years. In fact, figures from the government prove that the average income of black American families at the end of 1987 really was less than it was twenty years ago, in 1970.

You see, you really need a commitment, and that's what Coach McCartney has made at Colorado for the black athlete. He has taken a strong stand and as a result he has brought about an understanding, some healing, some fairness, some validation for the minority athlete.

He understands—and slowly but surely is making others see—that the average black athlete comes from a world view that is different. He comes from a place and time where there is less hope than ever before in the American dream. I'm of the belief that the increase in gang membership and the horrible increase in drugs represent the lack of hope for black America.

It always strikes me when I realize you have young people today, black and white, who know nothing of John and Bobby Kennedy, nothing of Johnson's social legislation,

(Continued)

nothing of Martin Luther King, Jr. I've taught these kids, and it's interesting to realize that they weren't even born when these great men were struck down. On the other hand, there are white yuppies who haven't benefitted from Kennedy's wisdom and leadership and who feel perfectly free to express their racial prejudices.

The system today simply doesn't provide adequate and equal opportunity, so you have more and more young people in the black community saying, "I can't make it legitimately, so I'll make it some other way." The issue is this: What are we doing about discrimination? I tell young people that there are certain rules of conduct they need to learn, understand and obey, and that when they are mad and upset, there are ways to react without resorting to violence and aggression.

Racism is both white and black. I see significant progress at Colorado, but things are not turned around in an instant. This football team has come together as one heartbeat. We believe in each other.

If I could use an analogy, Jesus Christ at the last supper spoke of sacrifice with the bread and the wine. It took the surrender of a grape to make the wine; the surrender of a kernel to make the flour for the bread You see, we're talking about remembering, bringing ourselves together as one in sacrifice and in love in order to celebrate the ultimate victory of man.

Sixteen

Temptation in Texas

I t was springtime in the Rockies in 1988. The Colorado Buffaloes had just completed three straight winning seasons. And life could not have been sweeter.

That is, unless a fellow had a chance to coach at Southern Methodist University. And I was about to get that opportunity.

SMU had gotten the NCAA's "death penalty" and couldn't field football teams in 1987 and 1988. But after a rash of recruiting violations and some of the most unfavorable publicity any university ever received, it was time for the Mustangs to get about the business of selecting a coach. I was interested in the job from the very start. SMU needed to rebuild, and I'd had experience in rebuilding the Colorado program—I knew I had made mistakes but I also knew I could profit from those blunders.

What a time to think about leaving! We'd had Colorado in two post-season bowl games in three seasons—and might well have had a third bowl bid—and we'd brought the Colorado program back to respectability. We had good, young players in the program and it was on solid footing.

But in my mind, here was SMU, a private institution of Christian background, beckoning to me. Sharing the Gospel is more important to me than coaching football, and the American Civil Liberties Union had forced the university to come down on me about praying with my players or sharing my faith with them. As a result, I was beginning to feel stifled.

From the time I had gotten into coaching, I understood all the hazards—or thought I did. I knew the best way to win friends and influence people was to go 11-0, win a major bowl game, be ranked number one and beat the point spread every game. Then I'd at least have most of the fans on my side.

But because I chose to speak out publicly about my faith—and because of the furor caused by an article in the Sunday magazine section of the *Boulder Camera* newspaper in December 1984— a certain segment of the population was never to forgive me, never to embrace me, no matter how many games we won or what lofty ranking we achieved.

The person who wrote the December, 1984 article, Janet Wiscombe, didn't misquote me at all. But hordes of people were very upset by what they read, thinking I was imposing my beliefs on everyone around me, including my players. And since not every player was receptive to me, more than one had said, or inferred, that since we were coming off a 1-10 season and had won only seven games in three seasons, it was obvious we had recruited more choir boys than football players.

The article was titled "God and the Gridiron" and it was front page stuff. Mix in the fact that Athletic Director Bill Marolt had extended my contract in the middle of that 1-10 season—when plenty of people were demanding that I be fired—and you have the makings of a messy situation.

The critics said I tried to evangelize the whole team, and I suppose they're right. It's my hope that wherever I'm coaching, whatever group I'm dealing with—football players or an audience of just plain folks—that I could persuade every single one of them to come to a saving knowledge of Jesus Christ. But playing certain players because they were Christians? Not on your life! Not once. Not ever. The best players played. I have never given Christian players preferential treatment.

I prayed long and hard about the SMU situation, and the answer I kept getting was that—with the Colorado program now on solid ground—it was time to move on.

What I was seeking was freedom: freedom to say whatever I wanted, whenever I wanted, without worrying that Judd Golden, the attorney for the ACLU, was going to follow up with his threat to file a lawsuit. Of course, SMU was attractive for other reasons, too. It had a rich academic tradition and the school had excelled in athletics—I knew that success could be recaptured without cheating.

Doug Single was the athletic director at SMU, as he'd been at Stanford and Northwestern. Before talking with him, I had privately discussed the SMU situation with some good friends of mine in the Southwest Conference, and they thought it would be an ideal situation for me. The faculty at SMU had been offended by cheating that had taken place in the football program—so much so that there were calls for cutting out football entirely. The SMU administration wanted excellence with integrity, and I knew I could deliver. I returned a call from Doug Single in December and told him up front that I was interested in the job.

But first, there was the not-so-small matter of my current contract at Colorado.

I had originally signed for four years when I came on board in 1982, signed an extension as we were winding down that disastrous 1-10 season in 1984, and had signed still another four-year contract and hadn't used up a year of it yet! The University of Colorado had been very good and very generous with me.

Shortly after my first conversation with Single, I went to Montgomery, Alabama to coach in the Blue-Grey game on

Christmas Day. While I was in Montgomery, I spoke several times with Doug, and we chatted further after I got back to Boulder. We agreed it was in our mutual best interests to keep our negotiations secret, and decided to meet in Dallas after I'd attended a coaches' convention in Atlanta.

Lyndi went with me to Texas, and I remember we had to sit on a runway in Dallas for four hours after we landed, because they'd just had the worst ice storm in the history of the city!

Single and the administration showed us around the city, and then around the campus. All was going well, until. . . One of the Dallas newspapers had a writer staking-out the SMU athletic offices. It was right out of some spy novel—I was in Single's car, slunk down low in the seat to keep from being spotted. But nothing worked. The writer had already spotted me, and stayed on our tail all the way. We were virtually certain that our cover was blown!

Lyndi and I stayed two days, experiencing nothing that would discourage us from making the move. We made arrangements to return to Dallas a few days later with our four children so SMU could formally introduce me as the new head coach of the Mustangs! We'd even determined salary, length of contract, and perks. SMU had every right to believe I was coming, even though I hadn't signed a paper nor even gotten a handshake on the deal.

I got through the Dallas airport without anyone recognizing me and thought perhaps our secret was safe, after all. I was not prepared for what greeted me when I deplaned at Stapleton Airport in Denver.

It seemed like every writer. . .every television reporter. . .every camera in Colorado was pointing at me. There were lights in my face. I wasn't fresh. I wasn't on top of things. I needed a shave and if I'd had a razor right then I might have shaved right above my shoulders. I didn't want to lie. What I wanted was to get out of there and say as little as possible, but everyone detected something in my demeanor that told them, "He's gone."

The following day, a Friday, I met with our coaches and told them I was leaving. Because of NCAA limitations at SMU, I couldn't take a full staff with me, so we talked back and forth about which coaches would go with me and which would stay. On Saturday morning, I remember waking up and telling Lyndi I thought going to SMU was the right thing to do; that I was being led there by God. And she agreed. I had resolved to meet with our athletic director, Bill Marolt, and with our president, Dr. E. Gordon Gee, a few hours later and tell them of my decision. I was nervous, but I was ready to explain the reasons for my decision.

It was a brisk, sunny morning in Boulder when we met in Dr. Gee's office. He isn't one to waste many words, and he went directly to the offensive:

"Bill, I don't want you to leave. I want you to stay right where you are. You made a commitment here. You signed a new contract. Furthermore, when you signed that contract, you asked me if you could depend on me to stay here at Colorado University. Not long after I told you I'd stay, one of this country's major universities invited me to be its president. It was a flattering opportunity, and I was seriously thinking about it, when my wife reminded me that I had made a commitment to you and to your program. So I quickly withdrew my name from any consideration. Now you tell me you're going to leave. I just can't accept that."

I'll say this, we didn't waste much time with small talk.

When he paused, I spoke up. "But this is something I feel the Lord has led me to do. I wouldn't do it if I didn't think it was God's will. That's my only motivation for leaving. I like it here. I'm not dissatisfied with my contract. We're going to have good teams here. It's just that the combination of going to a private, Christian school is very attractive to me."

He looked me straight in the eyes and said, "I just don't believe Almighty God wants guys to neglect commitments and break contracts."

I was lost for a response. I got up to leave, saying, "Let me think about this thing."

The entire session had lasted no more than fifteen minutes. I walked to my car, then drove to a Catholic church and went inside. The church was empty. I knelt down to pray and opened my Bible to the concordance in the back, looking for the word "commitment." And I was directed to Matthew 5:37 from the Sermon on the Mount: "But let your 'Yes' be 'Yes' and your 'No,' 'No.' For whatever is more than these is from the evil one." The verse seemed to speak directly to my heart. I prayed to find someone who wasn't involved in the decision, who had no prejudices and could help me make the right decision.

I went then to the First Presbyterian Church, looking for a minister named Bob Oerter. I'd heard him speak at a Fellowship of Christian Athletes gathering and was very impressed by his message and his eloquence. But I couldn't find him anywhere. So I went home and immediately telephoned Dan Stavely, a good friend and confidant and a mighty man of God. He'd been in coaching almost half a century, much of that time at CU. I had compete trust in him.

I put the whole thing right in his lap and he came right to the point with his reply.

He said, "I don't want you to leave, Bill. And it's clear to me that if you do, you'll be violating Scripture."

That did it. Simple as that. I knew then and there I could not leave Colorado. I immediately called Marolt and President Gee and told them I was staying on. The incident had caused so much controversy, they suggested we call a press conference. We had it that night in a conference room at the basketball arena and the place was packed. It was an emotionally trying time for me, and I was mightily affected by the people who were there and the outpouring of support for me and my family and our program. I had certainly put everybody through the wringer!

Incidentally, the decision to stay at Colorado didn't draw the same kind of reaction from Texas. When I called Doug Single and told him I'd changed my mind, he just lost it.

He screamed at me, saying he had called the other candidates and informed them he had a deal all set. He had planned to make

Sunday morning headlines in Dallas, but Denver and Boulder got the headlines instead. We struggled back and forth, Single insisting I had given him my word. I admitted that I had been ninety-nine percent certain I was coming to SMU, and that I'd told Doug Single as much. But I told Doug that I'd also said that I would have to talk with the Colorado people first. Nevertheless, I agreed that he had every right in the world to be upset with me.

When I think back on it, I had unhappy people all over the place. Yes, people had said nice things to me at the news conference, when I tried to explain that I didn't necessarily want to go to SMU but felt it was the kind of thing I'd been trained for. I had told them it seemed as if the time spent in Colorado had been to prepare me for something like SMU, where I could help resurrect and restore a program that had collapsed. And everyone had seemed understanding; supportive even.

But the next day, the focus in the news media was on what my vacillating had done to recruiting within the Colorado program—and the die-hard fans were upset. Naturally, people in Texas thought I had betrayed them—and I had. What I had promised SMU wasn't so out of line: sure, it was breaking a contract, going back on my word, ignoring a commitment. Yet coaches do it all the time. Players in the pro ranks are constantly violating contracts, holding out for more money and demanding—and getting—a renegotiation.

At the end of the 1989 season, Bo Schembechler announced he would be stepping down after the 1990 Rose Bowl game against Southern California. Even before Bo made the formal announcement, I got several phone calls, mainly from old pals in the Michigan media, asking me if I'd be a contender for the job. I gave each of them the same answer: "I have a contract. I will coach at Colorado in 1990 and will not be a candidate for the Michigan job nor any other position." Almost as soon as Bo stepped down, when he was still athletic director, he named our mutual friend Gary Moeller as his successor. So it became a dead issue. But the point is that under no circumstances would I have considered the job, because I already have one and *I will never break a contract.*

I learned my lesson.

And what about it being God's will that I should go to SMU?

I think the Lord allowed me to go all that way to see if I would go there, if I would be obedient to Him, if I would give up a program definitely on the upswing for one that had collapsed. I know in that last critical period of time before my final decision was made—in the last twenty-four to thirty-six hours—there were a lot of strong people saying strong prayers, and if all of us were praying the right way, we were praying that God's will be done. I'm persuaded that it was.

You see, all sides have profited. SMU chose a fine coach in Forrest Gregg and the program did much better than anyone could have expected or hoped in its first season back playing football. And our Colorado program has thrived.

In trying to put things behind us, I continually stressed to anyone who would listen that I would be at Colorado for the duration of my contract, unless the university terminated me. Winning eight games the following season helped quiet the turmoil, and even though Brigham Young beat us in the Freedom Bowl—a game we should have won—everyone could see the Colorado program had momentum. And then came the Golden Season of 1989.

I intend to stay at Colorado University as long as I feel I can be effective, as long as the university wants me—and as long as I feel that it is what God wants Bill McCartney to do.

I really do try to stay tuned in to the will of God, and what God wants for me and my family is the most important consideration. I'm sure a lot of people don't understand me or my thinking. But it's pretty simple. My rationale is this: The number one reason every one of us is on earth is to make Jesus Christ famous. What

I want to do is to make sure I place myself in the situation where I can best be of service to Him.

There's an important lesson I learned from the SMU flirtation. It taught me that when you give your word—whether you sign your name or shake hands—your word must be your bond. It's the very same thing I say to young men I'm trying to recruit to play football at Colorado. "Do you understand what this commitment means—and that it's two-way?" I tell them. "If you broke your leg and could never play football at Colorado, we would still have a scholarship for you. But by the same token, I'm holding you to the word you've given me here, and I'm going to go out from here and make other recruiting decisions based on what you've told me. Because you've decided to come to Colorado, I'm going to say 'no' to somebody else. So please understand that you're giving me your word, okay?"

I'm happy to say that most young men are true to their word. Three out of four stick with their decision. But I understand those who make one decision, and then change their minds. After all, I've been there.

Seventeen

Nobody's Perfect

My co-author once wrote a book called *Nobody's Perfect*. And neither is college football.

If you read your morning paper today, or watched last night's newscast, there's the chance that you read or heard something unpleasant about sports. Perhaps someone's been caught doing cocaine, marijuana, steroids. Maybe a school did some illegal recruiting, paid some athlete under the table, let him use a telephone credit card, saw to it that he got an automobile, altered some transcripts. It could be some professional sports agent signed him prematurely, paid for a nice trip somewhere, even gave him some front money. Perhaps you read about some college athlete getting into a fist fight, a barroom scuffle, being drunk and disorderly. You may have felt surprise—even disgust—over the news. But you shouldn't have.

Unless you are raising young people in your home, nurturing

them through their formative years of high school and college and keeping close tabs on them to boot, then you cannot possibly have any idea of the choices and challenges facing them today. The temptations today's young person faces can in no way be compared with what students faced in decades past, when panty raids and chug-a-lugging were the primary campus rages. College years are formative years, when many young people are out of the nest for the first time in their lives. They are bombarded with more opportunities to build character—and to get into trouble—than ever before.

Of course, there are people who say that the college student, particularly the student-athlete, should be held to a higher degree of accountability, and higher standards, than your average bear. If we fall prey to this kind of thinking, I believe we are doing the athlete a terrible disservice.

Crime. . .immorality. . .scandal. . .drugs. . .if it happens anywhere in America, it'll happen on the college campus. These things are evil, terrible, despicable, hurtful—but they do occur. And they occur because sports, whether on the high school, college or professional level—is simply life in microcosm. We exist in a sinful world occupied by hedonistic people whose god is the almighty dollar. To expect teenagers, intoxicated with the new freedoms of college living, to hold themselves to a higher degree of accountability than the rest of society. . .well, it seems to me a pretty unrealistic expectation.

In the February 27, 1989 issue of *Sports Illustrated*, there were two articles dealing with the so-called evils of big time college football. One was called "An American Disgrace" and underneath the title were the words, "A violent and unprecedented lawlessness has arisen among college athletes in all parts of the country." The writer, Jerry Kirshenbaum, said that "universities are being robbed of their integrity." His criticism was widely and generously distributed among coaches, university presidents, admissions officials, professors and fans—and, of course, the players.

In the other article, the cannons were leveled at the University of Colorado. "What Price Glory?" it was titled. Beneath the title were these words: "Under Coach Bill McCartney, Colorado football has taken off, but so has ugly criminal behavior among the Buffalo players."

Rick Reilly wrote in his lead: "There are a few things a University of Colorado campus policemen won't leave the office without: handcuffs, his copy of the Miranda warning, and a University of Colorado football program."

Then he related instances where some of our athletes had gotten into trouble with the law. Some of the incidents have been serious. The university administration is not naive, as the writer suggested, nor do I fail to grasp the seriousness of it all, as he wrote. Anytime a player is accused of anything that is a violation of the law, it's of grave concern to me. Some of our players have been found

Tony Versaci:

Years after our years coaching together at Divine Child High School, Bill told me that the thing that stuck with him most about our program, is that there is almost no limit to how young people will respond if you show them you're fair and concerned about them as human beings and not just as athletes. Bill was always fond of saying that discipline is a special kind of love.

When I decided to leave my position as head coach at Divine Child, Bill had been with me three seasons, and there was no question about who'd take my place. And when Bill had the opportunity to join Bo Schembechler at Michigan, it was apparent that Bo saw in him what I saw: a moral, ethical man who was at once a very bright coach and an incorruptible human being — a winner by any measuring stick.

guilty; in other cases, charges have been dropped.

I seethed for six weeks over the article. I thought it was evil and scurrilous. When the *Westword* article appeared some months later, I downgraded the *Sports Illustrated* piece to merely spiteful and unfair. But it tore at my guts and kept me in an agitated state for so long that I determined the only thing for me to do was to disencumber myself. I decided to call Rick Reilly.

"I need to talk with you," I said as soon as I got him on the phone.

He seemed defensive.

I went on: "I want to ask your forgiveness for the hostility I've had in my heart for you."

"Well, okay."

And that was it.

That night I wrote in my daily journal:

> I asked Rick Reilly for forgiveness for what I had harbored. I meant it, but I'm afraid I didn't communicate much real love over the phone.

Maybe all that doesn't matter to Rick. But it was important for me, and that's enough. My motivation wasn't to get him to write something good about us. It says in the Bible that if you harbor anything against any man, you must put down what you have at the altar and go back and seek forgiveness. I had to reconcile things within my own heart.

I would not suggest to you for one minute that college football is without problems—and some big ones, at that—or that our Colorado program is trouble-free. I've suspended players for a game, for a season. I'll probably do it again. Players have complained to each other, to the assistant coaches and to me about playing time. They've quit the team because they weren't playing enough. They've threatened to quit because they're broke all the time, and they think—and I agree with them—that the NCAA ought to revise its rules to give athletes some kind of a stipend.

The problems that confront coaches and players generally are the same everywhere, in every program. There are some problems, however, that are unique to Boulder because of the fact that so many of our quality athletes are black and so much of the community and the university is white.

I consider Reilly's article in *Sports Illustrated* to be a gross misrepresentation of our program. But to his credit, I think it's significant that he pointed out that sometimes, it has seemed that some of the people of Boulder and some members of the police force have given our players a rough time.

The article also pointed out that in 1980, blacks comprised 1.5 per cent of the population in Boulder and less than two per cent of the Colorado University student body. Our academic coordinator, Theo Gregory, pointed out something in the article that I think is worth repeating here. He said: "If you're a black football player here [in Boulder], you're ethnically a minority because you're black, socially a minority because you're an athlete, culturally a minority because you might come from the projects, economically a minority because you can't afford to drive a BMW and physically a minority because you're bigger than everybody else. Somebody racially slurs you, and you might have a tendency to overreact."

I'll say this about student-athletes and altercations off and on-campus—there are a lot fewer problems in Boulder today than there were some seasons back.

And as for college football in general? I'm not at all persuaded that college football has as many problems as the critics suggest, and here's why: Every one of us has a reticular activated memory system and here's how it works. If you were going shopping for, let's say, a lawn mower, when you get on the street or in your car, suddenly you'll notice all sorts of signs and advertisements for lawn mowers. You'll see sales in the newspapers, billboards and you'll hear about sales on the radio and television. And it's all because you're tuned in. Your antenna is up, and you'll notice things you never made note of before.

That's part of what has happened with college athletics, with all the bad publicity it has received. Every time something unfavorable happens, it reinforces the opinion that the whole thing is a terribly evil endeavor, and that something drastic must be done about it. I don't believe that, and I'm right in the middle of everything that's going on. If I thought college athletics were evil, I'd get out of it right this minute!

The fact is, what I believe about college athletics is quite the contrary.

The late Bear Bryant was fond of saying that college football is the last outpost of discipline in the country today, the only place where a young man can go out and engage in a healthy and worthwhile endeavor, line up with all things being the same, and square off against the guy across from him. And once he's there, it doesn't matter what color he is, how much money he has, how bright he is. He simply has to compete on even terms with the same rules applying to everyone.

I believe football really is character forming. It's being part of a team; part of something bigger than yourself. It's still an arena where good things are taught, where sacrifices are learned, where a young person can perform often at such a high level of efficiency that he can outdo a man bigger than he. The military used to offer these important lessons about discipline and putting team ahead of everything else. The daily grind of football is very important, and so is the way a young man can look himself straight in the mirror when he knows he has given his very best in a worthy cause, one bigger than the individual.

Corny and old-fashioned? Perhaps. But you could say that about apple pie, too.

We'll always have stories about the troublesome athlete and

the unsavory coach, because they make "better" news. You don't have to remind me that when you deviate from what is normal, accepted behavior, *that's* when you make headlines. I understand and accept that.

But I do not understand nor do I accept the yellow journalism that is practiced by a small segment of the media. So many of the hopeful stories, the inspirational stories about the enriching experiences that most of us see—well, they're never brought to light. They're simply not considered "news." Ever since Watergate, there are a bunch of people racing around who think they're the new Woodward and Bernstein. Everyone is looking for the sensational story, the explosive situation. And yes, some of them do unethical things to try and uncover such stories.

In 1986, when we lost our first four games and then won our next five, there was a sensational story on the front page of the *Rocky Mountain News* claiming that there were drug problems on our football team.

There weren't, but the newspaper had gotten wind of a situation that had happened over the summer. They had built their story from information leaked their way by a campus police officer.

When our players had reported back for workouts that August, we had instituted a tough drug program with teeth. The athletic department rules were strict and severe—one positive test for drugs and an athlete would be suspended for a year. We instituted an elaborate and costly testing program that included sixteen drug tests a year at a cost of sixteen thousand dollars. We were determined to have a clean program, and one way to do it was to have strong deterrents.

During the summer, we had some young athletes who were experimenting with cocaine. Knowing we had tightened the screws in order to have the strongest drug program in the land, they agreed to cooperate with campus police so the police could uncover anyone who was dealing drugs on campus.

These young men had used drugs, but were not using drugs then. They cooperated with the campus detective, who interviewed them—off the record, they were told—and then took the information and spoon-fed it to a reporter.

These kids had no reason ever to suspect the information they had given, in confidence, would result in their names being splashed across the front page of a major newspaper. The inference was clear: The Buffs were a bunch of dopeheads! And then I had to face the same youngsters I had urged to cooperate; the same young men I had assured that whatever they said would be held in strictest confidence.

One more thing. About our "drug-riddled" program: out of sixteen thousand urine tests administered in the 1986 season, the Colorado Buffaloes did not have one positive test.

But that didn't make big, black headlines in any paper!

College football generates a lot of money at most schools. Television revenue is at an all-time high. In most cases, football supports virtually the entire athletic program. So I don't think finances should be a deterrent for what I'm about to suggest:

I'm recommending mandatory and extensive drug testing at every major school, for every athlete. I'm recommending a sound program of drug education for the athletes in the hope they'll be solid enough to stay clean. And if they don't, I think our automatic one-year suspension is not a bit too harsh.

Now, let's address a few other problems and controversies surrounding college football:

Freshman eligibility. Most young men are not ready, physically or emotionally or socially, to play football as freshman. But some are, and you can't discriminate against them. In 1989 we had five freshmen play out of a recruiting class of twenty-three.

Look at Notre Dame. You really have to give this school a lot of credit. Notre Dame recruits quality and graduates quality, most of the time in four years. This is a university that has proved you can win, and win the right way—and Notre Dame does it with freshmen, when they're good enough to play. But while they're playing football, they can't play games in the classroom. Notre Dame proves you can do both, do it well, and do it in record time. Some young men are mature enough and talented enough to handle it, and to deny them an opportunity to compete is wrong.

Athletic dorms. The first thing I did when I came to Colorado was to close an athletic dorm. In most cases, dormitories reserved for the exclusive use of athletes are nothing more than "Animal House" revisited. Athletes housed separately are denied the opportunity to interact with other students, and as a result often can't relate well to other members of the student body. This sort of isolation isn't good for anyone. The University of Colorado requires all freshmen to live in university housing. My personal rule is to require all freshmen and sophomores involved with the football program to stay in university housing. My experience is that young people need to be at school a couple of years and gain some maturity before they can handle their money wisely. If you give them a rent check—the equivalent of university housing —they're usually broke within ten days and wind up with severe problems with the landlord.

As for co-educational housing—I'd eliminate it altogether. What goes on there is really alarming. If parents had any clue as to the things that go on in the co-ed dorms in America's colleges and universities, they'd hesitate even to send their children to college. A young person who wants to live a clean, moral lifestyle finds it almost impossible to exist under those conditions, and undergoes heavy pressure to compromise the values so important in his life.

Agents. Like everything else, there are good ones and there are the sleeze-bags. The guys who are ruining it are the slimy ones who are trying to make a living without working. They latch onto promising athletes and make arrangements to wheedle a percentage of their income. Agents recruit college kids just like we do when we're scouring the high schools, and they promise them flashy clothes, entertainment, lavish trips and fast cars. They're often dealing with young people who may have come from the poorest of circumstances and who sometimes are captivated by all that glitz.

The athletes aren't blameless, though. If we're doing our job educating them, they should be better able to make sensible decisions. But their desire for the good life is easier to understand if you've sat in their homes and seen first-hand the poverty that exists there. I stress to our players that they don't need anyone to look out for their interests until they see whether they've been drafted by the National Football League, and their position in the draft order.

The death penalty. I'm all for it for schools who are repeat offenders, who keep on breaking NCAA rules. And I'm all for the death penalty for coaches. Why should a coach with a long history and tradition of excesses be permitted to work somewhere else? When SMU got the death penalty (no football for two seasons) it sent a ripple through college athletics that nothing else could have done. There is no better deterrent than shutting down a school's program, and the same thing would work in the coaching fraternity.

> **Many times your best athletes are black athletes and many times they are the products of a single-parent home where they may not have had guidance to make solid decisions. These young men and their parents are the ones most often seduced by false promises and influenced by slick but insincere talk.**
>
> *Bill McCartney*

Someone pointed out to me recently that in the past ten or twelve years, about half the winningest football programs have been cited for cheating. I find that more than tragic. More than absurd. It's unnecessary!

For eons, Oklahoma has been one of the most powerful football programs in the country and right now, Oklahoma is on probation. But Oklahoma doesn't have to cheat. Oklahoma's traditions are established. Oklahoma is very difficult to beat at the recruiting game when the Sooners really go after a young man. Without cheating, Oklahoma has what young men are seeking—a top flight school with an impressive record of athletic successes.

Stipend for athletes. I'm for it. When I went to Missouri on a football scholarship, I got room, board, tuition and fifteen dollars a month. Do you want to talk about the inflation of the dollar since the early sixties? To give athletes seventy-five dollars a month wouldn't hurt a thing. Today's athlete can ill afford to walk around the corner and buy a hamburger and a soft drink.

The super conference. Some major college coaches would like to see a so-called "Super Conference" made up of schools like Notre Dame, Penn State, USC, Oklahoma, Nebraska, Michigan, Ohio State, Auburn, Alabama, Miami, Florida State and so forth. It's not for me. We have a good product the way we are. Attendance figures are growing. Our conference affiliations are good. Let's not mess with it.

A national playoff. If Colorado had beaten Notre Dame in the Orange Bowl, we'd have been the national champion. Between the wire service polls and the present system of post season bowl games, we generate plenty of interest to last from August through the first of January. Of course, we don't always agree with the poll results—I know Lou Holtz of Notre Dame didn't agree with the last one—but the great thing about the whole deal is that we'll line up next season and go at it again. There's enough interest, enough attendance, enough everything. College presidents have said they're opposed to the playoff system and we need to support them on this. The people who run our colleges know a lot more about academic priorities and what's good for the student-athlete than do the fans who are screaming for the playoff. And, I might add, a whole lot more than the coaches.

Booster clubs. Time was when various colleges got into trouble with the NCAA for allowing their boosters to get out of control. Much of the trouble among the schools in the Southwest Conference took place because boosters and overzealous alumni ran wild. They want to win so bad that they'll do anything to get the job done. A few of them will even do things that are illegal, either out of ignorance of the regulations, or because of their win-no-matter-what-and-how thinking.

During the time I coached at Michigan, we took full advantage of the fact that the university has the largest alumni body in the world. We flooded recruits with strong letters from alumnae, extolling the virtues of Michigan. This can't happen under today's rules—alumni clubs and booster organizations have pretty much been stripped of their power. They're important to the coaching staff and there's nothing nicer than having strong support from people who are encouraged about your program, but the people running these organizations—as well as the coaches—need to maintain tight reins to guard against possible NCAA infractions. Booster clubs have to make sure members understand that they aren't allowed to have any contact with a recruit. Not so much as a single telephone call.

Not long ago, I had a telephone call from a perfect stranger. He knew we were recruiting a blue-chip performer out of the Denver area.

"I'm going to help you get _____ to come to Colorado," he offered.

I told him I appreciated his interest in our program, but that he could not help us one whit.

"I have a pal of mine who plays for the Chicago Bears and I'm going to have him call this young man, and then I'll take him over there and have him talk with the kid."

"Don't do a thing," I pleaded. "Anything you do will be a violation."

His disbelief was apparent even on the phone and I went on to explain how rigid the rules are. Here he was, a nice man merely trying to help our program. All he wanted to do was have his pal, who'd made it to the NFL, tell a high school senior that Colorado would be a nice place for him to attend.

Proposition 42. This one takes the place of Proposition 48, which stated that in order to compete as a freshman, an athlete had to have at least a 2.0 grade point average in certain high school courses called "core courses." That was designed to keep athletes from inflating grade point averages with things like gym and shop. In addition, the student had to accumulate eleven core units—and then had to score seven hundred or better in the SAT test or fifteen or better in the ACT test.

Under Prop 48, if an athlete didn't score high enough, he could still come to school on a scholarship but could not compete, or even practice with the team, for his freshman year. When Proposition 42 came along, it went one step further. Prop 42 had the same criteria, but determined that flunking the SAT or ACT meant an athlete could not be granted a scholarship his freshman year.

I liked Prop 48 better. I thought sitting out a year was ample punishment. There are some people who simply do not test well. Junior Seau was one of them. He came out of Sal Aunese's neighborhood and had a terrific grade point average, I think something like a 3.5, but he did not pass the entrance tests. We desperately wanted him to attend Colorado. We talked with his coach, his instructors, his counselors, and there was no question in anyone's mind that Junior would do well in college. Yet, he had to sit out a year at Southern Cal. I don't have his grades in front of me, of course, but I have it on good authority he's been a solid *B* student from day one.

The late Woody Hayes, unquestionably one of the all-time legends of college football coaching, once said he was in favor of bringing the very marginal student into a college situation even if it was apparent the young man had no chance of getting a degree. As much as I respect Coach Hayes for his record of accomplishment, I disagree totally with that concept.

Coach Hayes' line of reasoning was that a young man would benefit from the college experience, regardless of whether or not he graduated. I won't deny that can happen. At the same time, I think there's a very real danger that a young person could become so disillusioned that he is scarred for life.

I think a coach has a definite responsibility *not* to bring a person to a university where he cannot compete in the classroom. Picture this: you bring the extremely poor student into the college situation. He reports in August for football practice. He sizes himself up against the older athletes, does the very thing he was recruited to do and is pretty good at it. And everything's going all right—until school starts.

Suddenly this very marginal student, who is probably from a disadvantaged background and is possibly black, walks into the classroom and looks around to discover that almost everyone else is white including most of his professors. He listens for awhile and begins to realize he is out of place. Most everyone else can figure out what the instructor is saying, but he can't. And he is immediately intimidated. He says to himself, "What am I doing here?" Fear overtakes him. Unless this person is highly motived with an awesome drive to work and sacrifice, he cannot make it, no matter how much guidance, no matter the amount of tutoring he gets. You do him a disservice and the university an injustice, because you have given the athlete false hope and allowed him to take a spot that could have been given to someone more skilled.

On the other hand, if I see a young man who can be salvaged, who is reachable and teachable, and if my coaches and I—and the other members of the team—can give direction and hope to that person through goal-setting and hard work, then I want him on my team. If we provide the right tools and the proper environment, I'll take my chances that this young man will wind up being a positive force in the world and a contributing member of society.

What if we hadn't taken a chance on Sal Aunese? He was no honor student in high school. He was a Prop 48 kid: He couldn't pass the tests to be eligible as a freshman at Colorado; he couldn't even work out with the team in his first year at college.

But he came to us as a success-oriented young man. He'd been a huge star in high school. Scores of colleges and universities wanted him. Surely he could have gone to some school where his grades would have been handed to him. He chose Colorado. And he went to work, applying the same tenacity in the classroom that he did on the football field. He got eligible. And three games into the 1987 season, quarterback Mark Hatcher was hurt and Sal went in—and never came out. From then on, he was our first string quarterback.

> **Perhaps the most important thing any coach can do is to make himself available to his players; to make them understand that his door is open, that he sees them as individuals as well as a team, that they can talk with him.**
>
> *Bill McCartney*

But during the following off season, Sal ran into trouble with the police and spent twelve nights in jail. He'd had a few beers with some pals, and they were walking down a sidewalk between two dormitories. Some kid on the third floor had been drinking heavily and yelled some obscenities, some racial remarks, at Sal and his buddies. Sal challenged the guy, telling him he'd be right up.

When Sal got to the hallway where the guy lived, he found the door locked. Sal should have left well enough alone, but he didn't. When he was sure he had the right room, he banged the door with his shoulder and did some damage to it, but still couldn't get in. And he still didn't leave. Sometime later, he found the door open and the student lying drunk of the floor.

Sal straddled him, growling, "Look. You want trouble?"

The student was in no position to defend himself, and wisely shook his head *no*.

Sal never laid a hand on the guy. He'd had his satisfaction, and he left.

And for that, he spent a dozen nights in jail. It was grossly unfair punishment. But I had no choice but to take disciplinary action, too. I suspended Sal from spring practice.

But Sal served his time, took his punishment, like a man. He didn't lash back at me, nor anyone else that I know of. Sure, he thought the police had been unduly harsh, and I do, too, but he knew he had been in the wrong. When he came back for fall practice, he was in good shape and so were his grades. He picked up right where he'd left off. He still had the respect of his teammates and he reassumed his leadership position.

Sal Aunese was a winner. He had his frailties. Sometimes he failed. But I could not say then, nor now, that he was a young man of flawed character.

When he was stricken with the cancer, he was on his way to becoming one of the most celebrated football players in the country. More importantly, he was on target to graduate. Most important of all, he not only handled his illness with the same courage and grace he displayed on the field, but before he died, he gave Jesus Christ control of his life to gain the most important victory of all.

Eighteen

Countdown to Miami: The 1990 Orange Bowl

We arrived in Miami on December 22. When it comes to bowl games, there are almost as many theories—on when to travel, how many days to spend at the game site, how strenuous practices should be—as there are coaches to espouse them. We arrived in Miami two hours behind schedule, so I called off the practice scheduled for that afternoon. Notre Dame coach Lou Holtz was quoted as saying he thought we had arrived too early. Former Oklahoma coach Barry Switzer said our schedule was just right. I'd been to a lot of bowl games with the Michigan team, and Bo Schembechler never seemed to keep the same schedule two years in a row (the Wolverines couldn't seem to shed the so-called "bowl-jinx" and Bo got to where he was willing to try almost anything), so I didn't take the speculations regarding our timing too seriously.

My next decision, after cancelling our first practice, was to close our practices to the media. Immediately the headline in the *Boulder Daily* Camera on December 24 trumpeted:

Paranoia Sets In for McCartney in Miami

The *Denver Post* added, "The shroud of secrecy surrounding Colorado football practice was worthy of a top secret NASA space launch."

I've always tried to be very accommodating to members of the media—in fact, lots of people say I talk *too* much to the press and volunteer a lot more information than I need to. But right then, mere days before our contest against Notre Dame, my first responsibility was to our team. I wanted to give them the best preparation possible, and that required a lot of concentration and intensity.

Not that there wasn't time for a little comic relief. One of our former players turned graduate assistant, Chris Symington, played Santa Claus at our squad Christmas party, assisted by little T.C. in a Santa costume, too.

Miami was going through such a record cold snap that I doubt any of us would have been shocked to look out the window and see a white Christmas. It was too cold even to walk the beach, although the weather finally sneaked into the fifties and about thirty of our players braved the icy Atlantic waters.

Notre Dame had arrived on Christmas night, and Coach Holtz immediately began campaigning for the winner of our game to be voted number one. One of the Notre Dame players, tailback Ricky Watters, belittled Colorado's schedule and said we didn't deserve the top ranking. I avoided commenting since I didn't want to give any more ammunition to a Notre Dame team already loaded with talent.

Besides, I knew the game Holtz was playing.

All season long he'd been downplaying his own team's ability, trying to lull the opponents to sleep. Only days before our game he was saying to anyone with a microphone or notebook, "We're just not very good."

In the days leading up to the big game, most of the media

attention was on Lou. That's the way it should have been—and the way I liked it. While Lou was accustomed to the national spotlight and obviously reveled in it, it was my baptism. And besides: I don't do magic tricks.

Only days before the game, Lou moaned that his game-breaker, Raghib (Rocket) Ismail, probably wouldn't be able to play. That shoulder dislocation he had suffered in late November in the Miami game just hadn't healed, the kid hadn't really practiced, he'd experienced no contact and well, as a matter of fact, he just might have to be floated into the Miami harbor aboard the U.S.S. Hope.

Just as players should never underestimate opposing players, coaches shouldn't be taken in by what we'll call coaching rhetoric. Okay, so Lou Holtz does magic tricks. So he's a funny after-dinner speaker. So he kids about wearing glasses, having the same body configuration as Woody Allen and speaking with a lisp. This same Lou Holtz has done coaching wonders wherever he's been. He's the only coach to take William & Mary to a bowl game. . . garnered the best four-year record in North Carolina State history. . . coached nationally ranked teams at Arkansas. . . turned the Minnesota program completely around in just two years. And at Notre Dame, in just three seasons, his team won the national championship.

All of us knew those were no accidents. No one could dispute Holtz's coaching talent. And I never worried that our players would be over-confident.

Three days before the game, Coach Holtz's remarks in front of his squad on the Orange Bowl field were splashed across national headlines. You'd have thought the FBI, the CIA and the KGB had infiltrated Miami!

A cameraman from a Denver station had been shooting background footage and his field microphone was still "hot" when Holtz began addressing the Notre Dame players during a pregame practice. Holtz said, referring to a *USA Today* telephone poll that named Notre Dame the popular choice as the nation's best college team:

"The bad of it is that Colorado feels they're being slighted. They're gonna be sky high and they don't get any respect, and all that other nonsense. The good thing is, it sends a message to everybody who votes, that after we win the football game, they can't do anything else but put Notre Dame number one. They can't, believe me. . . They're used to scoring a lot of points. They ain't playing any Kansas State. We got to be patient on defense. Just play our football game. On offense, we want to control the football. All we want is a first down, first down, first down. Frustration will set in on Colorado's offense. By the middle of the third quarter, they will leave the game plan completely and start grab-bagging. Remember me telling you that. They are not patient. Their quarterback will want to make plays and we aren't gonna let him. Stop the bomb. Control the quarterback."

Holtz also said about our team: "They're living a lie. They've been living a lie all season."

I really don't know what Coach Lou was talking about—and it didn't really matter then and it doesn't matter now. He had a perfect right to say everything he did, and I find no objection to any of it. I don't think it should have been made a national issue, but that's part of the pre-game hype that is automatically attached to such a game. Someday, though, perhaps Lou will tell me what he meant when he said we'd been living a lie.

I'm sorry his quotes were made public. It's my feeling that a coach's remarks to his players are private and should be kept that way. Lou apologized the next day and I told him the matter had already been forgotten, that no apology was needed or expected. I've been in coaching over a quarter of a century, and I've never met the coach who'd want his on-the-field or locker room talks—and surely not his sideline comments during the heat of battle—aired before the general public. It was a cause celebre that had no business happening, and wouldn't have happened under normal circumstances. But when hundreds of media people descend on an event like this, everything seems to race out of control.

Everything that had already been written and said by everyone was being written and said all over again. Every step of our program and personal lives was fair game again—from the day I arrived on campus full of hope and expectation, to the dark days of the early failures, to the fullness of the police blotter, to my daughter's pregnancy and Sal Aunese's cancer and Sal's other girl friend, to comments from someone that I was decent and candid and caring and concerned and wonderful, to a quote from someone else that I was slightly tetched—believe me, not a single detail was spared in the search for one more story, one more angle. I'm confident, however, that during our eleven days in Miami, I said nothing that would get me into *Bartlett's Familiar Quotations*.

No one came to me, either, with any deals to bellow "I'm going to Disneyland!" after the game. Our plans were firm—we'd go back to Colorado at nine the morning after the game. We had come to Miami to do a job, and when it was over we'd go home, simple as that. I told Dick Connor of the *Denver Post*: "If we win the game, I'm going to remember how we prepared, what we did, how we did it. If we lose, I'm going to reflect on what we did wrong, what we should have done differently. Preparation is totally subject to second-guessing."

During the last days of preparation, both Lou and I had to deal with contract issues that came out of nowhere. Even though I had a year to go on my contract, I was asked about whether I'd seek or demand or accept a contract extension, as well as if I had my eye on another job. Holtz was busy answering one of those so-called "inside" reports that he was about to pull up stakes at South Bend. Thank goodness the game was just around the corner, else they'd have had one or the other of us joining some hippie commune, or worse.

Going into that New Year's night, I thought about the fact that, tomorrow, it would be a Notre Dame team that had won eleven national championships going against a Colorado team doing it for the first time—a Colorado team emerging from a tough conference that some had called the Big Two (Oklahoma and Nebraska) and the Little Six (Colorado, Iowa State, Missouri, Kansas, Kansas State and Oklahoma State).

On the eve of the Orange Bowl game, we arranged for the team and the coaches to stay at a hotel near the airport, just to escape the carnival atmosphere and to try and focus on the game plan. That night, I wrote in my journal:

> My thoughts this day go to you, O Lord. You are my focus, my desire, my enthusiasm for life. This game is exciting, people make it exciting and heighten its importance. Yet, Your stamp upon it broadens its values. I want only to serve You, Lord. You fill my life with Your Spirit. Time with You enlivens me.

I'm not suggesting for one minute that God sits on His throne and decides which team is going to win a particular football game, nor that He even cares. What I am saying is merely this: That I want His anointing on me; that I can pray to my God that He will touch every player on our squad and bring him to a saving knowledge of Jesus Christ.

And that, alone, will create winners, no matter what the outcome of any game on any athletic field.

On the morning of the game we held mass and a chapel service for the players who wanted to attend. About fifty players came to the service, which was conducted by Pastor James Ryle. I went to both sessions, and during chapel Pastor Ryle and I shared with the players the dream he'd had that had foreshadowed the incredible events of the past months; his dream of our Golden Season.

That morning, the first morning of the new year, the headline writers in Colorado had penned:

CU Girds for National Title Shot
No. 1 Questions: Will Buffs Sizzle or Fizzle?
Irish May be in Disarray for Showdown with Buffs
Buffs on the Lam—CU Goes Underground
Buffs Look for National Title
Buff-Irish Battle a Game of Inches
Colorado Won't Falter in Orange
Colorado Must Maintain Poise to Win
Buffs Take Aim at National Title
Only a Colorado Victory Will Terminate the Debate
Colorado Easily Favored in Poll

The poll, incidentally, was done in Colorado and found seventy-four percent of those surveyed said they thought we'd win. While I'm thrilled there was that much optimism about our chances, I'm glad our players didn't see the poll before the game. I believe our players went into the game with enough confidence in themselves and in our game plan.

None of us—not a player, not a coach—was intimidated by the thing everyone calls the "Notre Dame mystique." The week of the game, Coach Holtz was asked about that very thing and his response was that you really couldn't define it, but on the other hand, you could sense it, feel it and be certain it was there.

Colorado had no mystique going for it. We had a group of young men who had traversed a difficult road, who had overcome a ton of adversity and emotional upheaval and who were physically prepared for victory.

As we boarded the buses that would take us to the game site, I was filled with excitement. . .confidence. . .determination.

As the buses pulled up to the stadium, we were met by a horde of Colorado fans, their excitement bordering on hysteria. I was, I think, happier for them than I was even for our squad. This was what Buff fans had hoped and prayed for, through so many frustrating years. They had lined up eight deep—and they had their game faces on, believe me! And that infected our team, to a man.

Maybe we were too high, because when we had those early

scoring opportunities and failed to get a point, the fall was a mighty one. At halftime, our players were very subdued. I felt they had lost their confidence and gotten into a position where they didn't really know if they could beat Notre Dame. Of course, I didn't say that as we regrouped in the locker room between halves. Rather, I stressed that Notre Dame hadn't really stopped us; rather, we had stopped ourselves.

When the clock ran out and we had lost, I guess the feeling I had more than any other emotion was one of exasperation.

I was dejected that we had let this opportunity—one you rarely, if ever, get—slip away. But I knew I would not make excuses, nor alibi for our performance, and I didn't want our players to do it, either. They'd had a terrific season, and the first thing I told them when we all got into the locker room, was to hold their heads high.

The headlines on January 2 read:

Irish Spoil Colorado's Dream
Notre Dame Uproots Colorado 21-6
ND Ends Buffs' Title Bid
Buffs Self-Destruct

The streamer across the top of the Rocky Mountain News seemed to say it all:

Heartbreak

Then there was one other headline that was very telling:

Healthy Rocket Picks Up 108 Yards, MVP Trophy

Raghib (Rocket) Ismail carried the ball sixteen times, picked up 108 yards and the most valuable player trophy.

It's a game we could have won and should have won. Three times in the first half we were knocking at the door. Early in the game our tailback, Eric Bieniemy, was all alone inside the Notre

Dame twenty-yard line and decided to switch the football from one hand to the other, and. . .well, he just dropped it, that's all. No one hit him. No one even touched him. Notre Dame recovered. In the second quarter, we put on a really fine drive from our own eighteen-yard-line to Notre Dame's five—and could not score. Ken Culbertson tried a fourth-down field goal—a chip shot, really from twenty-two yards—and it sailed left. The only other time he'd missed from that distance was when his attempt was blocked.

But this was a team with heart. The headline writers were correct—we did self-destruct. But we did not quit. We did not lose heart. We marched down the field once again in the first half and had a first-and-goal from the Notre Dame one-yard-line—and still could not score. You simply cannot give a team like Notre Dame that many opportunities.

We could have been leading 17-0 at the half—but the world is full of could-have-been, should-have-been, might-have-been stories and people tire of hearing them. There's a quote by Oliver Wendell Holmes that I like: "To brag a little, to crow gently when you win, and to own up, pay up and shut up when you lose are the virtues of a sportsman." The plain truth is that the game was there for us to win and we didn't do it.

But it's not the end of the world. Not for our players. Not for our great university. Not for the great state of Colorado.

I'm proud of not only the way our young men played, but also for the way they conducted themselves during and after the game. No one offered any excuses. Eric Bieniemy tried to shoulder all the responsibility—"I blew it, plain and simple," he said. He was way too harsh on himself. Here was a young man who could well lead the nation in rushing during the 1990 season. But he was playing against Notre Dame in his first game since mid-season. He'd been out with a broken leg and it's a tribute to his will that he came back at all.

A writer for the *Miami Herald* said in his story: "If it had been written in Hollywood, maybe it would have been different." It was, he said, a storybook season without a storybook ending.

When it was over and the players were milling about the locker room, some of them expressed great disappointment that we hadn't won just one more game for Sal Aunese. Others said it was still a dream season.

Regrets? Sure, I have some. But apologies? Not a one.

I think our coaches prepared the team well, and the players played well. It was the opportunity of a lifetime, I had said after the game, and we let it slip away. Had I been a little more thoughtful, I instead would have called it "one of the opportunities of a lifetime." It was merely the end of a season, not the end of the world. Football is temporal. It is transitory. Yes, the object is to win and I want to win every time I compete, regardless of the game. But these are games played on a field, and the stories are written in press boxes and news rooms, not in Hollywood.

Some years ago, a Big Ten coach said, "Defeat is worse than death, because you have to live with it."

That's one of the most ludicrous statements I've encountered.

A defeat is just that—a defeat—and nothing more. It is a setback, not a humiliation; it is a reversal, not a tragedy. Someone wrote that the game gave Colorado respect. We didn't go there looking for respect because we had it when we boarded the plane in Denver. We got it all season long the same way winners get it, by earning it, rather than screaming and stomping and demanding it.

I stand by what I told our players after the game.

I said that I was proud of them and that I wished I could have done more to prepare them to win the game.

Nineteen

A New Tradition of Excellence

W hen we got back to Colorado the day after the game, it was gratifying to see several hundred fans there to greet us. Even the governor showed up. And all of us sensed the same thing: that this was the not end of one season but the beginning of a new era in Colorado football.

The *Boulder Daily Camera* said in an editorial:

> To call the last five years "a turnaround" would be to dismiss Colorado's achievements with casual understatement. No other college or university in the nation so completely transformed its football program in the last half of the decade.

We had learned how to win. We had learned how to live with adversity and to overcome it. We had learned how to be a team.

We had learned that high achievement is attained only through sacrifice. We had learned what my late father's hero, Franklin Delano Roosevelt, meant when he said that the world does not want the kind of man who shrinks from temporary defeat; rather, one who rises again and wrestles triumph from defeat.

The *Daily Camera* editorial used the right words:

"This was not an isolated, emotion-charged season; it was the end of a rebuilding process and the beginning of a new tradition of excellence."

After the defeat in Miami, someone interviewed my son Marc, who volunteered the opinion that I would suffer long and hard because of the loss. Marc cited the way I had responded to our loss the year before in the Freedom Bowl against Brigham Young.

"He'll sit in his room all day tomorrow and the next day and he won't come out," Marc was quoted. "After we lost to Brigham Young, he barely talked for two weeks. And this game meant so much to him."

> **Nothing that was said after the game alters one whit of what took place during it. We lost. On that night, Notre Dame was a better team and deserved to be ranked number one.**
>
> *Bill McCartney*

Marc was right on two counts: The Orange Bowl did meant a great deal to me, and I had taken the loss to Brigham Young very hard.

When Colorado lost to Brigham Young, I was bitterly disappointed. I didn't handle that defeat well at all. Yes, I did pray after that setback, but I also sulked and pouted. I was like a fighter who had come back to his corner after taking a tremendous pounding and confronting not only my opponent's strength, but my own weakness. Back then, I didn't come out fighting like the champion that I want to be, the champion I have trained to be. In the words of Roosevelt, I shrank from temporary defeat.

But this defeat was different.

I was different.

From the night before the Orange Bowl game until January 6, 1990, I didn't write a word in my daily journal. When I did finally put something down, I said:

> Didn't feel like doing the journal for a few days. Dealing with the defeat okay. Helps to get out on the recruiting trail and get back to work. Visited six young men in Los Angeles. Losing the game doesn't appear to have hurt our recruiting. My feeling is that we will be back for big stakes in the future.

You see, I had changed, too, from the year before, just as our players had changed. I, too, had a new outlook—a new spirit.

The fifteen-month journey from that night when Kristyn told Lyndi and me she was pregnant had taken all of us through calamitous times that had tested not just our patience but our faith. We had experienced the miracle of new birth and the snuffing out of a young life; the public degradation of my daughter; the denunciation of our players and our program, and the vulgar mockery of my Christian beliefs.

There was a new maturity in me, a spiritual growth that gave me perspective and left no wallowing in the loss of a football game.

A lone defeat did not tarnish our golden season.

Painful? Yes. Permanent damage? No. A defeat in a football game is not the end of the world. Life goes on.

And if you work it right, it goes on eternally.

In late February, we committed to a twelfth regular season game on our 1990 schedule. We agreed to play Tennessee in a season kick-off game at Anaheim on August 26. No one pushed me into saying yes; in fact, our official family at Colorado left it strictly up to me. I said yes mainly because I knew it would be a unique opportunity for our players to be challenged right from the start. And I think it will mean a thirteen-game schedule this season, because I firmly expect the Buffaloes to be in a major post-season bowl game.

On March 8, I gathered all our players together for the first time since the Orange Bowl, and I began to challenge them from day one.

I reminded them that we need to anticipate a thirteen-game schedule, something no Colorado team has ever done. No Colorado football team has ever won back-to-back Big Eight championships and we must prepare to achieve this as well. And this year, Colorado won't be sneaking up on anyone. We'll be expected to perform at a much higher level and thus, we have to expect much more from ourselves as individuals and as a team.

I told them that our greatest resource is that we have twenty-five seniors and that gives us the right to expect quality leadership from our older players.

It was a where-we-are-going and how-do-we-get-there kind of

> **God enables us to be winners. But He requires so very much of us in order to accomplish it.**
>
> *Bill McCartney*

talk. And then we set some goals: 1) Win the Big Eight championship and go to the Orange Bowl and 2) Win the Orange Bowl.

Finally, I reminded our young men what the late Vince Lombardi had said. He said there is one characteristic that all truly great teams embrace, and that is simply that they all operate on one heartbeat.

A year ago, when we lost the Freedom Bowl game to Brigham Young, I was sorely embarrassed. Not because we lost, but because we weren't a team. We had more talent than did Brigham Young, but we had played as a bunch of individuals, and it cost us the victory. At that time, I had determined that I would never again be part of any operation so fragmented.

As I faced this group of young men that adversity and hard work had begun to forge into a team, I told them about the giant redwood tree. I explained that the tree can grow to three hundred feet at maturity, yet the amazing thing is that its roots rarely grow deeper than six to eight feet in the ground. How does it stand? How does it endure even the slightest breeze? As I told my players, redwood trees grow in clusters—their roots embrace, intertwine, grab hold of each other and never let go.

Our team would have to come together like that.

"The higher we climb," I told them, "the harder the wind blows."

We would have to be ready.

I knew we had already started networking, growing together, standing clustered and not alone. The *team* concept had first manifested itself in our third game of the 1989 season, just before Sal's death. We were slated to play against Illinois. Both teams were ranked and undefeated. We defeated the Fighting Illini and later, in the locker room, I saw Erich Kissick celebrating more wildly than any of our other players. He was our captain, a fifth-year fullback who had started every game in the previous season. He was yelling and jumping all over the place, carrying on like a little kid. I went to him and said:

"Erich, do you realize that you didn't carry the ball even once in this game? You never touched the ball. You're our starting fullback, yet the second string fullback carried the ball ten times."

Erich kept right on celebrating. You see, he was so caught up in the success of the team that he lost track of individual records and personal achievements. I immediately called that to the attention of the other players.

"That's the kind of guy I want at the helm, as the captain, in the leadership position, because he's so wrapped up in *team* that he forgot about *self*."

We had an even greater challenge the following week, after Sal's death. No one could anticipate how we'd respond on the field following the numbing loss of Sal. But we won decisively, and then discovered anew that we had at last grasped the real meaning of the team concept. Earlier that week, running back Eric Bieniemy had been listed as one of a half dozen or so top Heisman Trophy candidates. Yet he carried the ball only eight times for eighty-two yards and J.J. Flannigan carried fourteen times for eighty-five yards. But Eric celebrated without caution—it didn't matter that his chance for the Heisman had dimmed. He was caught up in *us*. When our team gathered on the field before that game, our players—who had been looking to Sal's spot in the stands as a rallying point—pointed a little higher, toward the heavens, as a tribute to Sal, and I knew we were for real. We were, at last, a football team.

We had gone through so much together. And that had drawn the circle tighter. Some people wondered why we were saluting Sal so much. A few cynics suggested we were overdoing it. I told them simply that Sal was an ordinary guy with extraordinary leadership qualities, and that while he was somewhat like other people on our team—a guy with faults, a decent student, a fellow who was in and out of mischief—he was also a guy who more effectively personified the selflessness required for high achievement, and for high achievement as a *team*, than any other player I knew.

In the 1990 season we will face Tennessee in Anaheim, Missouri in Columbia, Illinois at Champaign, Texas in Austin and Kansas in Laurence—all tough road games climaxing with Nebraska in Lincoln. These games will require that we be as tough mentally as we are physically; that we sacrifice self for *us*; that we stand tight, that we link skills, that we operate on one heartbeat.

These games will determine whether we can recapture the magic of 1989—and exceed it. In addition to our determination to be mentally tough, we have adopted as our theme for 1990 the slogan "Trust in me." Every player on the team has to be able to look every other guy in the eye and say with conviction: "You can trust in me. You can count on me. You can depend on me to prepare, to practice and to perform with the best interest of the team in my heart."

It's not really all that different in the world outside football, is it?

Bill McCartney:
Biographical Sketch

Date of Birth:
August 22, 1940

Education:
Graduate of Michigan's Riverview High School, 1958
Graduate of University of Missouri with a degree in
    education, 1962

High School and College Athletic Record:
Earned 11 letters in football, basketball, baseball in H.S.
Captain of H.S. football and basketball teams
Received football scholarship from University of Missouri
Earned 3 letters as center-linebacker at University of Missouri

Career Milestones:
Assistant football coach at Missouri's Joplin High School, 1964
Basketball coach and assistant football coach at Michigan's Holy
    Redeemer High, 1965-68
Football coach at Michigan's Dearborn Divine Child High,
    1969-71, coaching basketball and football teams that won
    state titles
High school head coaching record: 30-5
Named assistant coach at University of Michigan, 1974
Named defensive coordinator at University of Michigan, 1977
Named head football coach at University of Colorado, 1982

Following the 1989 season, McCartney was named:
Kodak Coach of the Year by the American Football Coaches Association; Bear Bryant Coach of the Year; Walter Camp Foundation Coach of the Year; Sporting News Coach of the Year; UPI Coach of the Year, and Big Eight Conference Coach of the Year.

Personal:
Married Lynne (Lyndi) Taussig on December 29, 1962
Children: Michael, Thomas, Kristyn and Marc
Grandchild: Timothy (son of Kristyn)